JEWS &
CHRISTIANS
in Pursuit
of Social Justice

JEWS &
CHRISTIANS
in Pursuit
of Social Justice

Randall M. Falk
Walter J. Harrelson

ABINGDON PRESS
Nashville

JEWS AND CHRISTIANS IN PURSUIT OF SOCIAL JUSTICE

Library of Congress Cataloging-in-Publication Data

Falk, Randall M.
    Jews & Christians in pursuit of social justice / Randall M. Falk,
Walter J. Harrelson.
      p.   cm.
    Includes bibliographical references
    ISBN 0-687-01122-1 (pbk.: alk. paper)
    1. Judaism and social problems.   2. Church and social problems.
I. Harrelson, Walter J.   II. Title.
HN40.J5F35   1996
261.8—dc20   96-16203
                                                                          CIP

96 97 98 99 00 01 02 03 04 05—10 9 8 7 6 5 4 3 2 1

MANUFACTURED IN THE UNITED STATES OF AMERICA

For our grandchildren

Marnina Rose Falk
Naomi and Rachel Falk Logan

Heather and Heidi McIver
Ansel, Jessie, and Clea Harrelson

with the prayer that their generation may further the realization
of a just and enduring peace for all children of the One God of
humankind.

CONTENTS

INTRODUCTION

Jews and Christians share a great historical and literary foundation in the Hebrew Scriptures. From this precious heritage come the basic moral truths, the ethical imperatives, and the social concerns that profoundly influence our personal lives and our community outreach. It was not until the second century of the common era that the early Christians added to their sacred Scripture the New Testament. In the early third century, Jews found in the Mishnah, edited by Judah ha-Nasi, interpretation and amplification of Hebrew Scriptures that enabled the Diaspora Jews especially to understand the application of the Law to their living situations. Although the New Testament and the Mishnah brought forth many divergent theological concepts, based on Hebrew Scriptures, the moral and ethical teachings of Judaism and Christianity remained essentially the same in these anthologies of religious instruction.

The purpose of this book is to examine the literary bases for Jewish and Christian impact on the individual and communal moral and ethical issues of our day. We recognize, of course, that within both the Jewish and the Christian communities there are differences in interpretation and application of both our traditions to many of the current moral controversies. We shall try to present the divergent interpretations in both Judaism and Christianity. It should be understood, however, that each author will emphasize his own stance on the issues to be confronted. We believe that we have the responsibility to articulate clearly our own application of our religious convictions to the social concerns of our times, and at the same time express our recognition and respect for the differing stances of other teachers and spokespersons within our respective traditions.

INTRODUCTION

This book, like our first one, *Jews and Christians: A Troubled Family*, began in a seminar that we taught together for students in the Vanderbilt University Divinity School and in the Graduate Department of Religion. Our goal, both in the seminar and in this current volume, it to undergird the conviction that Jews and Christians have a special contribution to make to discussions in the realm of social justice. We bring to these issues of moral and ethical concern not merely our individual concepts of right and wrong, but also the collective wisdom of more than 2,800 years of the quest for an understanding of how we can respond to the challenge of the prophet Micah: "What does the LORD require of you,/ but to do justice, and to love kindness,/ and to walk humbly with your God?" (Mic. 6:8). We believe that an understanding of this heritage will enable us to speak with conviction on specific issues and to fulfill our covenant with God: to live by God's teachings in order to come ever closer to the establishment of God's rule on earth.

We are deeply grateful to the many persons who shared in producing this volume. Our students in the graduate seminar did much of the research on many of the topics presented here. Charles H. Hambrick, Professor Emeritus of Religious Studies at Vanderbilt University, provided wise counsel for our chapter on "Jews and Muslims." Eve Wahl and Martha Young were most helpful and patient secretaries, typing and retyping the manuscript. Most of all, we thank our wives, Edna Falk and Idella Harrelson, for their encouragement and their sound counsel in the development of the subject matter to be included in this book.

Many of those who have used our first volume on *Jews and Christians* in college classrooms and in continuing education programs in churches and synagogues urged us to bring out this second volume. To them, too, we are most appreciative.

CHAPTER ONE

MARRIAGE AND FAMILY VALUES

A JEWISH OUTLOOK

The LORD God said, "It is not good that the man should be alone; I will make him a helper as his partner." . . . Therefore a man leaves his father and his mother and clings to his wife, and they become one flesh. (Gen. 2:18, 24)

In the second chapter of the book of Genesis, we find the basis for the primacy of the marriage relationship. This is the foundation upon which family stability is established and through which the family becomes the primary social unit in a democratic society.

If you were to ask what is the secret of Jewish survival through four thousand years of persecution and of wandering from land to land, an answer would be the security and the stability of the Jewish home, based on the relationships of husband and wife, parents and children, and their overall relationship to God and to God's moral law. We shall first examine these relationships in Jewish tradition and then seek to understand the ways in which they established standards of behavior both within the home and in the larger community.

While women were not regarded as the equals of men in biblical and rabbinic literature, there is ample evidence that women were treated with greater respect in Jewish life than was evident in most cultures in those times. The thirty-first chapter of the book of Proverbs (vv. 10-31) delineates the role and the responsibilities of the wife in a Jewish household. Although this may well be an idealized picture of women's status, this tribute to the Jewish woman is indicative of the high regard in which she was held.

The basic material and conjugal rights of women were carefully set forth both in Hebrew Scriptures and in the Talmud. Even the rights of slave women were protected, as evidenced in the book of Exodus (21:1-11). The concubine also was given proper consideration, as is seen in Abraham's concern for Hagar when Sarah required that Hagar and her son leave the household. Even though polygamy was not formally abolished in Jewish communities until the tenth century of the common era (when Rabbi Gershon ben Judah of Mainz and his synod forbade polygamy in France, Germany, and Italy with the penalty of excommunication if this edict were violated), the Bible stigmatizes as adultery any extra-marital relationship involving either partner. In Judaism, adultery was recognized as a deep moral sin, an offense against God, not to be atoned for by mere financial compensation.

In Jewish life, preparation for marriage began with a formal recognition of the engagement of a couple, known as *Kiddushin*. As the Hebrew word implies, this was a ceremony sanctifying the relationship of the man and the woman. Among the provisions set forth in the Kiddushin was the statement that the prospective bride entered into an exclusive relationship with the prospective bridegroom from that time forth. The scribe Ezra permitted pre-marital relationships between the engaged couple, though the rabbis in the Mishna were in disagreement on this issue. The rabbis in Judea permitted extra-marital relationships for engaged couples, but the rabbis in the Galilee did not. Eventually the stricter law of Galilee became the law.

Marital rights and responsibilities of men and women are set forth in a formal marriage contract (a *Ketubah*) as prescribed in the Talmud. The amount of the dowry a woman is to bring to the marriage is set forth, and the gift from the groom of a ring of specified value is also required. In addition to the material obligations, the Ketubah includes the conjugal rights of both men and women. The husband is required to satisfy the sexual needs of his wife as well as to provide for her material needs. It is clear that the sexual relationship is for the pleasure of both parties as well as for procreation. The rabbis taught that intercourse on the Sabbath was an integral part of Sabbath joy. Finally, though, the Ketubah also includes provision for mutually agreed upon payment from the husband to the wife, in case of divorce.

Family planning has been an integral part of Jewish life from earliest times. Although the first commandment in the book of Genesis is "Be fruitful and multiply" (Gen. 1:28), some rabbis in the Talmud maintained that the birth of two children would fulfill the Law. Some rabbis in medieval times disagreed with this ruling because of the high rate of infant mortality that prevailed in the ghettos.

Family planning in Talmudic times also included a very rational approach to birth control. In his fine book *Love and Sex: A Modern Jewish Perspective,* Robert Gordis cites a number of Talmudic passages in which rabbis permit birth control. The classic statement, repeated several times in the Talmud, tells us that "Rabbi Bebai recited a Tannaitic passage in the presence of Rabbi Nahman. Three types of women use an absorbent (to prevent conception), a minor, a pregnant woman and a nursing mother; the minor, lest she become pregnant and die; a pregnant woman, lest her embryo be injured and become a (fish-shaped flat) abortion; and a nursing mother, lest she wean her child too soon and it die."[1] We should also add that many rabbis permitted the use of birth control methods when the life of the mother would be endangered by a pregnancy.

The same kind of reasoning is found in rabbinic statements regarding abortion. An instance of therapeutic abortion is found in the Mishnah, where we read: "If a woman is having difficulty in childbirth (so that her life is endangered), one cuts off the embryo, limb by limb, because her life takes precedence over its life. (However), if most of the fetus (or the head) has emerged, it may not be hurt, for we do not set one life aside for the sake of another" (*Mishnah Oholot* 7,6). In his commentary on another passage from the Mishnah, Rashi adds: "The life of the mother in childbirth takes precedence over that of the embryo to the very last moment of pregnancy" (*Sanhedrin* 72b).

Gordis summarizes the arguments for and against abortion by stating that "abortion should be legally available but ethically restricted, to be practiced for very good reasons. Men and women must be persuaded that though the abortion of a fetus is not equivalent to taking an actual life, it does represent the destruction of potential life and must not be undertaken lightly or flippantly."[2]

1. R. Gordis, *Love and Sex: A Modern Jewish Perspective* (New York: Farrar Straus Giroux, 1978), 128.
2. Ibid., 147.

Probably the most troublesome issue that challenges Jewish family stability today is the matter of divorce. Evidently this was true even in biblical times as well. In the book of Deuteronomy (24:1-4) we find the first mention of a "certificate of divorce," which a husband may present to his wife simply if she fails to "please him" or he finds something "objectionable about her." At the same time that divorce seemed to be relatively easy, the next verse indicates that strenuous efforts were made to secure a marriage, even to the extent of allowing a recently married man to be exempt from service in the army for one year for the sake of the household, "to be happy with the wife whom he has married" (Deut. 24:5).

Needless to say, in matters of divorce, as in most interpretations of Jewish law and tradition, there is great diversity among the sages of Hebrew Scriptures, as well as between the rabbis in the Mishnah. For example, on the one hand the prophet Malachi states that God refuses to accept the sacrifices of a young man who has broken faith with the covenanted spouse; the prophet concludes, "Do not let anyone be faithless to the wife of his youth. For I hate divorce, says the LORD, the God of Israel" (Mal. 2:15b-16a). On the other hand, the scribe Ezra seems to encourage divorce in the case of mixed marriages between Jews and Samaritans. Some four centuries later, there continued to be differences among the rabbis regarding acceptability of divorce. The classic example of such differences is that Shammai taught that a man could lawfully divorce his wife only if he could prove adultery on her part. Hillel, however, taught that a man could divorce his wife for relatively minor reasons, even if she did not cook well. And Rabbi Akiba went so far as to suggest that a man might divorce his wife if he found another woman more attractive. Most rabbis, including Jesus, felt that only fornication or the failure to produce children (regarded then as solely the fault of the woman) were sufficient grounds for divorce.

Divorce became a matter of concern for the rabbis from an ethical as well as a financial perspective. The *Get* (divorce decree) can be issued only by the husband before a *Bet Din* (a rabbinic court); however, the rabbis provide a long list of causes on the basis of which a woman might also sue for divorce before the rabbinical court. Many of the grounds for divorce accepted by the more liberal rabbis like Hillel and Akiba may seem superficial or unimportant, but these

14

rabbis contended that these seemingly insignificant causes were evidence of a deeper clash between husband and wife that indicated that the sense of community of spirit had ceased to exist. When a marriage has failed and all attempts at reconciliation have proved futile, Judaism has regarded divorce as legitimate, as an admission of the failure of the marriage. This understanding of the validity of divorce for a variety of reasons is set forth quite clearly in Mishnah *Gittin* (9:10). Robert Gordis summarized the attitude of liberal rabbis toward divorce very well when he wrote:

> Once it becomes clear that the marriage is beyond remedy, Judaism recognizes that the union has lost its sanction and its sanctity, for love and mutual respect are the only marks of God's presence in a home. When these conditions do not obtain, the husband and wife are no longer joined together by God in any meaningful sense, and society stultifies itself by trying to ignore the truth.[3]

Jewish tradition has always shown a special sensitivity to the needs of the single woman and the single parent. Much has been written in Hebrew Scriptures and in the Talmud regarding the community's responsibility to the widow and the orphan. Providing for their physical sustenance is a basic obligation, but providing for the education of the orphaned person was of equal importance. Consideration of the needs of the widow is evidenced in the laws of levirate marriage found in many places in Torah, but delineated most carefully in the book of Deuteronomy (25:5-10). Essentially, levirate marriage provides that if a man dies and the widow is left childless, the next of kin of the deceased husband is obligated to take the widow as his wife, at least until she has born a child, so that there would be someone to care for her in the later years. Levirate marriage remained a requirement in Jewish life until the tenth century C.E., when polygamy was forbidden by rabbis in most countries where Jews lived.

A more difficult problem was that of the *Agunah*, the woman whose husband had deserted her or was lost in war or who refused to grant her a "get" for one reason or another. Some rabbis in talmudic times did maintain that if a husband was thought to have been killed in war or had deserted his wife for reasons unknown, the

---

3. Ibid., 120.

marriage could be declared void after seven years of no contact, and the woman could remarry. However, the prevailing thought among orthodox rabbis even today is that a woman cannot remarry without a "get" unless she is a widow. The Conservative movement in Israel has adopted some more liberal practices in providing for remarriage where a "get" is not obtainable. This has not been a problem for Reform rabbis, since Reform Judaism recognizes civil divorce and does not require a "get."

One of the most vexing problems in marriage for the Jewish people, since biblical times, has been that of mixed marriage, or intermarriage. The first mixed marriage recorded in Hebrew Scriptures was that of Moses to Zipporah, the daughter of a Midianite priest. Whether Zipporah converted to Judaism is not certain. We do know that Miriam, the sister of Moses, did not approve of the marriage and was punished by God for refusing to accept Zipporah as Moses' wife. The real problem of intermarriage does not surface in the Bible, however, until Ezra's return from Babylonian exile to find many Judeans married to Samaritans and having had children with them. Ezra tries very hard to remove the Samaritan wives and their children from Judea and thus separate them from their Jewish mates. While Ezra may have had some success in this undertaking, there was strong protest against his edict, which can be found in both the book of Ruth and the book of Jonah in Hebrew Scriptures. The major theme of a universal God of all peoples was an effort to refute the narrow particularism of Ezra and his followers by the authors of these biblical books.

Beginning in some of the books in the Apocrypha and continuing through the Mishnah, the emphasis changes to a matter of conversion. There is no question that Jews were active missionaries, at least until the time of Constantine, who recognized Christianity as the official religion of the Roman Empire and forbade conversion activity on the part of any other religious group within the empire. Most rabbis accepted converts as fit mates for Jews, and some of the rabbis even concluded that the converted Jews were to be honored above the homeborn, for they had chosen the responsibilities and obligations of Jewish life. The problem of intermarriage without conversion did not occur, however, until modern times. We shall discuss this as one of the unsolved dilemmas in Jewish life today later in this chapter.

Up to this point, we have discussed only the husband-wife relationship as basic to our concern for marriage and the family. Equally important in Jewish life is the relationship of parents and children. We begin with Abraham and his acceptance of the obligation to circumcise his son and to provide a suitable wife for him. In Exodus we find the commandment that children honor their parents. This is reiterated in the Holiness Code in Leviticus; in this third book of the Torah we also find emphasis on the role of parents as disciplinarians to make certain that their children obey God's Law. Not until the book of Deuteronomy, however, do we see the parents as the first teachers of their children. In the sixth chapter of Deuteronomy, parents are admonished to teach the words of God diligently to their children in the home. Parents were also expected to establish moral standards for their children. The Midrash cites a beautiful example of this in declaring that when the wife of Potiphar the Egyptian tried to seduce Joseph, her husband's servant, Joseph was tempted to yield to her because of her charm. We are told, however, that just at the crucial moment the image of his father, Jacob, appeared to Joseph. The moral standards in which he had been reared asserted themselves, and Joseph was able to resist the Egyptian woman's overtures.

In the Mishnah, the rabbis broadened the list of paternal obligations. The father was responsible to redeem his son from captivity (if he had been taken prisoner in war), to teach his son Torah, to teach him a trade, and to teach him to swim (in order to preserve his life). We note also that when there is a divorce and there are still young children in the home, the divorced wife must return to her father's house, but the children must remain with the father as his responsibility.

Throughout Hebrew Scriptures and, indeed, in all of Jewish tradition, children are regarded as a blessing. No matter what the financial circumstances of the family may be or what problems may arise in the husband-wife relationship, the welfare of the children is of prime importance. The desire for offspring is expressed in many of the books of Hebrew Scriptures, perhaps best summarized in the words of the psalmist:

Sons are indeed a heritage from the LORD,
   the fruit of the womb a reward.
Like arrows in the hand of a warrior
   are the sons of one's youth.
Happy is the man who has
   his quiver full of them.
He shall not be put to shame
   when he speaks with his enemies in the gate.
                                        (Ps. 127:3-5)

Having explored some of the foundations on which many Jewish marriage and family values are based, we shall now seek to relate these values to some of the more pressing problems in Jewish marriage and family life today. Divorce continues to be one of the major threats to the perpetuation and enhancement of family life. Although most rabbis today follow the more liberal attitude toward divorce of Rabbi Hillel, the rabbis understand nevertheless that the rising rate of Jewish divorces, not very far below the national average, is symptomatic of the erosion of values, which threatens to destroy the family by subverting the institution of marriage. Modern rabbis are trained in pre-marital and post-marital counseling, and early diagnosis and treatment of marital problems can be helpful. The real education for marriage, however, must begin in our childhood homes, where the sanctity of marriage should be emphasized.

Closely related to the problem of divorce is that of the single-parent family. The majority of single parents are women, who face the responsibility of raising the children with little or no help from their father. At the same time, these single parents have to enter the workforce to sustain their family unit. In addition, the single-parent families have often been uprooted from family ties in their home communities and find it difficult to develop a support group or to counter the loneliness that frequently accompanies single parenthood.

The synagogue and the church should be prepared to undergird the single-parent family in many ways. The congregations can provide extended family support and can organize single-parent groups for educational and social purposes. Most important for the congregations is the changing of the family image in the religious school and in the congregation itself to give the single-parent family status within the community. As we noted earlier, Jewish tradition has always been compassionate to the needs of the widow and the orphan. This must now translate into our concern for the women and children who constitute most of our single-parent families.

The role of women in the Jewish family and the Jewish community has changed in other ways as well. Many women today wish to continue to be active in the business and professional world after marriage and after adding children to their family unit. This means that the role of the husband-father must also change, so that the couple may share the caregiver role and household responsibilities. It also means that one of the valuable services the synagogue and church can offer is good, professional day care from infancy to kindergarten age within the congregation's facilities. This can be an important contribution to family stability. Ideally this service needs to be offered across economic, racial, and religious lines as a community undertaking.

Most women today are insistent on their freedom to choose how they wish to use their bodies in both achieving and limiting pregnancy. Orthodox rabbis still oppose birth control and abortion, because these violate the law to "be fruitful and multiply." While some Orthodox rabbis will make exceptions to the rule in cases where the woman's life is endangered by a pregnancy, this does not change their basic opposition to anything that deters procreation. This stance also is closely related to the question of when life begins. Though the majority of rabbis in the Talmud opted for the view that life begins only when the fetus is separated from the host, many Orthodox rabbis today maintain that life begins at the time of conception or when the woman first feels life within the womb. Conservative and Reform rabbis are much more liberal in these areas. Contraception is accepted as the choice that a couple may make in order that intercourse may be, as emphasized in the Talmud, not only for procreative purposes, but also for the pleasure both partners experience in this important aspect of the marital relationship.

In this consideration of marriage and family values, one more vexing area of conflict and concern remains. The issue of intermarriage also finds sharp differences between the religious branches in Jewish life and within those branches. We must be clear, at the outset, that intermarriage is that marital relationship in which one spouse is Jewish and the other non-Jewish. If the non-Jewish partner has converted, it is no longer an intermarriage. All branches of Judaism accept converts and regard them on the same level as those who are born Jews. Only where the partners in the marriage are of different faiths (this is the case in more than half of the marriages in which a Jew is the bride or groom) is there a serious problem. No Orthodox or Conservative rabbi will officiate at an intermarriage or consider the children of those marriages to be Jewish if the mother is not Jewish. The majority of Reform rabbis will not officiate at intermarriages, although a minority of Reform rabbis will do so. More important, the Reform movement has developed an outreach program, the purpose of which is to make intermarried couples comfortable within the Jewish community and to encourage them to educate themselves and their children in a Jewish way of life. In both the Conservative and the Reform movements, there is also the movement to welcome non-Jews into full participation in Jewish life.

Another important matter of choice in family relationships today concerns the rights and the status of gays and lesbians in our communities. In this area there is sharp difference between Orthodox and Reform Judaism in our attitudes and relationships with homosexuals. For the Orthodox, it is clearly stated in Torah (Lev. 18:22; 20:13) that homosexuality is an abomination and that two men found engaging in sexual activity together may be put to death. Although the rabbis seem to have little to say about homosexuality in the Talmud, the rejection of gays and lesbians as members of Orthodox congregations, denying them the privileges and respect given all other men and women, prevails to this day.

Reform Judaism has taken a radically different position. Believing that all human beings are created in the image of God and are equal in God's sight, Reform Jews accept homosexuals as full members of the community. In 1974, Reform Judaism was the first American Jewish movement to accept into its ranks congregations with an outreach to the gay and lesbian community. Approximately fifteen such congregations are now members of the Union of American Hebrew Congregations (UAHC); a member of one of these congregations is an elected member of the Board of Trustees of the UAHC. In its 1987 and 1989 resolutions on gay and lesbian Jews, the UAHC urged all of its congregations to encourage lesbian and gay Jews to share in worship leadership and all congregational life, to continue to develop educational programs in the synagogue that produce understanding and respect for homosexuals, and to employ people without regard to sexual orientation.

In 1990, the Central Conference of American Rabbis (CCAR, the Reform rabbinical organization) after four years of soul-searching debate overwhelmingly endorsed the following statement: "The committee urges that all rabbis, regardless of sexual orientation, be accorded the opportunity to fulfill the sacred vocation that they have chosen." However, a majority of the committee reaffirmed that "in Jewish tradition, heterosexual, monogamous, procreative marriage is the ideal human relationship for the preservation of species, conventional fulfillment, and the preservation of the Jewish people."

It is still too soon to know what impact these statements from the CCAR will have on the rabbinate and on the congregations in the Reform movement. We do know that the Hebrew Union College-Jewish Institute of Religion, the Reform rabbinical seminary, as a matter of record will accept students who are openly gay or lesbian. We also know of at least two primarily heterosexual congregations that are now served by gay or lesbian rabbis, in addition to a number of gay/lesbian rabbis now serving congregations oriented toward a gay/lesbian clientele. Much, of course, remains to be done to "normalize" the heterosexual/homosexual relations within the Reform movement. Rabbi Alexander M. Schindler, president of the UAHC, expressed the sentiment of many Reform rabbis and laypersons, when he said, in his presidential address at the 1989 biennial convention of this international organization:

In most mainstream congregations, we have not extended our embrace to include gay and lesbian Jews. We have not dispelled the myth of the "corrupting homosexual," of the counselor and/or teacher who would fashion children in his or her sexual image. And we have not consciously included gay and lesbian parents as part of the Jewish family circle. . . .

In our denial, in our failure to see one another as one family—indeed as one holy body—we forget Jewish history, we opt for amnesia. We who were beaten in the streets of Berlin cannot turn away from the plague of gay-bashing. We who were Marranos in Madrid, who clung to the closet of assimilation and conversion in order to live without molestation, we cannot deny the demand for gay and lesbian visibility.

In all of this, I am working to make the Reform Jewish community a home: a place where loneliness and suffering and exile ends; a place that leaves it to God to validate relationships and demands of us only that these relationships be worthy in God's eyes; a place where we can search—together—through the written Torah and the Torah of life, to find those affirmations for which we yearn.[4]

The Conservative movement is not ready to follow the Reform decision to ordain openly homosexual rabbis, nor do they agree that it is wise to help form separate homosexual congregations to be included in their movement. However, Rabbi Robert Gordis, who was one of the leading scholars and spokesmen for the Conservative movement, wrote:

There can be no question that homosexuals are entitled to more than justice before the law. It is not enough merely to remove the various kinds of legal disability and overt hostility to which they have long been subjected. Whatever evaluation is placed upon their condition, be it moral, medical, or psychological, they are human beings, our brothers and sisters, who deserve compassion and love from their fellow men and, above all, from their brothers in kinship and in faith.[5]

Many differing perspectives on this sensitive subject remain not only between the movements in Jewish life, but within these movements as well. It is important that we continue to explore ways in which barriers can be removed and mutual respect prevail among those Jews of differing sexual orientations.

Another decision within the Reform movement that has been quite controversial, but has been most helpful to interfaith couples who wish to raise their children as Jews, was the CCAR resolution on patriarchal descent. This maintains that since in biblical times descent was through the father—a pattern that changed only in the second century B.C.E., when Roman soldiers, after raping Jewish women in Judea and then deserting them, made patriarchal descent

4. A. Vorspan and D. Saperstein, *Tough Choices: Jewish Perspectives on Social Justice* (New York: UAHC Press, 1992), 203.
   5. Gordis, *Love and Sex*, 160-61.

difficult to ascertain in many situations—the ruling of the rabbis to follow matriarchal descent was a liberalizing of the law for valid and practical reasons. Therefore, accepting the choice of the parents to follow either patriarchal or matriarchal descent for the child they wish to raise as a Jew may be acceptable within Jewish tradition.

This discussion of marriage and family values in Jewish life, past and present, does not exhaust our various areas of concern today. Rather, it highlights those issues of greatest concern in the Jewish community. Other problems must be dealt with, such as child and spouse abuse, zero population growth, and full equality for women in many areas.

There is no question that the Jewish family is in crisis. Traditional values are being sharply modified, and the environment in which we live requires adjustments in our attempts to cope with the realities of family and communal living. The challenge to strengthen the family in America today is also the challenge to undergird what has always been regarded as the very cornerstone of democracy.

SUGGESTED READING

Gordis, R. *Love and Sex: A Modern Jewish Perspective.* New York: Farrar Straus Giroux, 1978.

Steinsaltz, A. *The Essential Talmud.* New York: Basic Books, 1976.

The Torah: A Modern Commentary. Commentaries by G. Plaut and B. Bamberger. New York: Union of American Hebrew Congregations, 1981.

Vorspan, A., and D. Saperstein. *Tough Choices: Jewish Perspectives on Social Justice.* New York: UAHC Press, 1992.

MARRIAGE AND FAMILY VALUES

A CHRISTIAN OUTLOOK

INDIVIDUAL AND FAMILY IN THE BIBLE

Christian ethics is firmly grounded in Jewish ethics, although with the coming of the Christian community and its spread throughout the Mediterranean world, a distinctive Christian ethical outlook soon developed. The Jewish component of Christian ethics continued to be of decisive importance for the moral life of the Christian community. For this reason, Rabbi Falk and I will frequently cover some of the same points, with some differences showing up but with much that is continuous in our two treatments.

THE IMPORTANCE OF THE FAMILY IN CHRISTIANITY

The family is of critical importance for Christian life, just as it is in Judaism, even though, as in Judaism, numerous moral and religious demands are directed to the individual. It is impossible to say with certainty whether the Bible intended that the individual come first and the community second. The first creation story in Genesis 1 clearly speaks of humankind as consisting of male and female, belonging together and together creating the central family unit, with the command to be fruitful and bring forth children to complete the family.

The creation story in Genesis 2 would seem to indicate that the individual, a male, came first and then the second individual, a female. Some recent discussions of this old narrative suggest, however, that the initial creation was not of a first "male," with a female to follow, but of what we might call a humanoid, not yet fully differentiated as to male or female. Then, while this first human entity slept deeply,[1] God operated upon it to produce the elements of the nuclear family, a male and a female human being, each of whom is drawn to the other to form "one flesh."

Clearly, the later creation story in Genesis 1 speaks of God's creating humankind, male and female, as a single act of creation, and there God places the blessing and the command upon the two of them together. We can be sure that in both of these stories of the creation, the human self is never meant to be an isolated individual. Life in community is the intention from the first.

It is striking that there is no suggestion in either of these creation accounts that the lives of the man and the woman are incomplete apart from children. It is true that in Genesis 1 the command to be fruitful and multiply is strongly affirmed. But in Genesis 2, the "family" consists of the LORD God and the first human pair living in the garden, caring for it and enjoying it. God is a daily visitor, and nothing suggests that this family, for the sake of its completeness, must have children.

Christian family ethics today needs to recognize this point. While children are a blessing from the LORD for the Christian as well as the Jewish family, the Jewish and Christian heritages both affirm the importance of the life of the individual under God and of two individuals bound together in love, each completing the existence of the other. We begin with Jewish and Christian family ethics, but neither Jewish nor Christian ethics overlooks the claim of God upon the individual, and neither insists that without children a loving family is incomplete. Genesis 2 closes with an idyllic picture of family life: two individuals, naked and unashamed, giving and

1. The Hebrew term *tardemah* is the same term used of the sleep into which Abraham falls after he has prepared the dismembered animals. The LORD then passes between these pieces as Abraham lies prone, the result of which is the creation of a new covenant bond between Abraham and the deity. In effect, God affirms by oath that should the promise to Abraham not stand, God is willing to suffer the fate of those dismembered animals. The point is that the use of such a numinous image as *tardemah* seems to suggest that both male and female are the direct result of a mysterious and fresh operation by God upon this first-created entity. See Genesis 15.

receiving love from each other and from the deity who joins them in the cool of the evening to share their lives.

This reminder is valuable at the start of our work. Many individuals today live alone, unsupported by spouse and children. Many couples also live without the gift of children. We must not place such stress upon the family as to suggest that our religious heritage has no word for the childless couple or for the individual who chooses to live alone or whose circumstances require a life alone. But without doubt, family ethics is the right place to start a discussion of the ethics of Judaism and Christianity.

DISTINCT FEATURES OF CHRISTIAN ETHICS

The Christian community, unlike the Jewish community, does not have a set of fixed practices concerning betrothal, marriage arrangements, and the marriage ceremony itself. Several texts in the New Testament offer important counsel about life within the Christian home.[2] These texts were drawn from both Jewish and non-Jewish sources, as Christianity spread throughout the Mediterranean world and beyond. Therein lies a major difference between Jewish and Christian family ethics. For the Christian community, a very great deal depends upon the social setting within which the Christian individual and the Christian family live. It is remarkable to note how much Christianity takes from the Jewish world, but it is also noteworthy that the Christian community focuses on certain critical elements within the Jewish world and on certain critical elements in the revelation brought by Jesus and elaborated by Paul and the other apostles. In other respects, Christian ethical practices and social customs draw much more heavily from local environments than has generally been the case within the Jewish community.

Just as circumcision, for example, is laid aside in the Gentile Christian communities and has as its sign the act of Christian baptism, so also betrothal and marriage practices quickly are adopted from the Greek, Roman, and other cultures within which the Christian church is planted. The ethics of the New Testament is itself a blend of well-known ethical practices of the Greek and Roman worlds and of the Jewish heritage. A part of this difference lies in the

2. See Ephesians 5:21–6:9; Colossians 3:18–4:1.

fact that Christianity has its "otherworldly" side; according to Paul, the church is a "colony of heaven" located here on earth. Our true home, Christians are taught, is the spiritual home into which we have already entered by baptism and are even now enjoying to some extent as we claim the divine presence among us by the Spirit and as we commune with the saints in heaven. Sometimes, of course, this side of Christianity has been stressed so heavily as to lead Christians to ignore, or at least to neglect, their responsibilities for life in this world. Such views also were used all too frequently by Christians in power to maintain their status in the world even as they consoled their enslaved or impoverished fellow Christians that there would be a better life for them in the world to come.

It would be a great mistake, however, to suppose that personal and family ethics within the Christian community was ever entirely otherworldly. Christian faith, like the faith of the Jewish community, is firmly rooted in this life, in this world, for it is this world in its entirety that God loves, cares for, and is claiming afresh as God's own through the life and witness of the faithful on earth. This means that Jewish ethics as rooted in the Jewish Scriptures is claimed in its essential features by the Christian community. Christian family ethics, therefore, has to do with the needs of the members of the family, with the responsibilities that each member of the community is to exercise in relation to the others and to the family as a whole. Essentially, then, Christian family ethics is at its heart firmly grounded in Jewish ethics, as tempered and illuminated by Jesus' teaching on Christian life and love (see the next section, "Christian Ethics and the Age to Come").

Like the Jewish family, the Christian family tends to give the place of major authority to the male head of the family, although in early Christian texts (such as Ephesians 5–6) the effort is clearly being made to show the mutuality that should obtain within the Christian family. While wives are to obey their husbands, we are told, husbands are to love and cherish their wives. While children may be disciplined, the discipline must not be so severe as to break the human spirit. And while slavery is allowed in these early Christian communities, it is given a major challenge, according to the texts that speak of the unity of the entire community under God and of the equality of each member before God.

These spiritual and ecumenical texts are of immense value for understanding the norms of personal family ethics within the Christian community. They belong with those texts from the Sermon on the Mount and elsewhere in the teaching of Jesus as reported in the Gospels. All of these make it clear that Christian personal and family ethics, like the whole of Christian ethics, is grounded in the claim that God has called into being within the church a community that is to be characterized not only by what Moses and the prophets and sages taught—central though that is—but also by the life God purposes to have in the Age to Come, when the divine promises will be fulfilled as a whole. The Christian community is thus positioned firmly on earth but draws its life and power and impulses, by the Spirit, from the Age to Come, from that time of fulfillment of life's purposes that is already encroaching upon our own time.

CHRISTIAN ETHICS AND THE AGE TO COME

"Be perfect!" That is the call of the Gospel, and, of course, it will not find easy realization within the Christian or the Jewish community. But nothing short of the life God purposes is finally acceptable—either to Israel's prophets or to Jesus and the apostles. This means that Christian personal and family life is lived out under two perspectives all the time. The first is the set of obligations that the Christian community, influenced and guided both by Jewish and by non-Jewish moral understandings and admonitions, works out and calls its members to adopt for life in this world. These concrete demands are found in Jewish legal texts, in prophetic texts, and in the great collections of Jewish wisdom literature. They also are found in the teachings of Jewish rabbis, collected and preserved in the Mishnah, as Rabbi Falk has pointed out. The covenant between God and Israel calls the people of God to maintain a wholesome life in community, respecting the life and goods and needs of all members, both within and outside of the family.

The second perspective of the Christian moral life is much more elusive and subject to much more controversy in interpretation, for it has to do with what kind of personal and family life best reflects life in the Age to Come, life as God purposes it to be for all the peoples of earth. By this second standard, Christians, as individuals and within the family, are called to a form of life in the world that many will consider self-defeating if not downright silly. They are to give way to the needs of others rather than to insist upon their own desires and needs. They are to avoid conflict and strife with neighbors and with members of the family. They are to practice Christian love, a form of love that continuously and relentlessly seeks the good of the neighbor rather than one's own good, a form of love that is ready to undergo loss and pain and suffering for the sake of others, even including the enemy. The Christian Gospels portray this form of personal and communal life as characteristic of Jesus, and it thus becomes the model of the moral life of Christians.

Clearly, Christians as individuals and as family members cannot know in detail what Jesus would do under ever-changing circumstances and within the radically changed forms of Christian life today. But it is not impossible to see how the spirit of self-giving love and concern for others that marked the life of Jesus can offer guidance in any circumstances that are imaginable. The problem is to hold together these two dimensions of Christian personal and family ethics, so that neither the individual nor the family is led either to despair over inevitable failures to measure up to the ethical demands of the Age to Come or to turn this ethic of the Age to Come into a purely spiritual thing. Christians all too often have been content, it seems, to leave God's good but damaged world behind, unchallenged by Moses and the prophets and no longer the locale of God's redeeming presence. Or they have found a way to live in the world, exercising good morals and prudence, being good citizens, but in the realm of Christian personal and social ethics finding it hard to do more than spiritualize the ethics of the Age to Come.

As we will attempt to show in our last chapter, the need seems to lie in finding a way to claim afresh the pictures of this Age to Come that have been drawn by Israel's prophets and poets and have also been elaborated in Christian literature and thought. Often these pictures of the coming fulfillment of God's purposes have simply been dismissed as visionary and of no major import for Jewish and Christian ethics today. It is better to take them with great seriousness. The Age to Come is that time beyond normal time when God brings to consummation all of the purposes that were at work in the divine creation, all of the aims and plans of God for the entire universe. Jewish and Christian prophets and seers have left us, in many and varied literary forms in the Bible, the fruit of their visions of that coming consummation of God's work. The early Christian community, whether we can fully accept its claim or not, was affirming that many of the features of this picture drawn by Israel's prophets had broken in upon the world in Jesus' own life and words and deeds, in Jesus' suffering and death, and in God's raising Jesus from death as the sign of the divine triumph over all darkness and evil and discord. They were not offering a new, non-Jewish hope for the world, but a new version of Israel's hope in God's ultimate plans and purposes for the world, a version tied to Jesus' own understanding of that hope and tied also to their experience of God's presence in Jesus during his lifetime and in the Christian community after the Resurrection. I believe that a fruitful area for Jewish/Christian study and dialogue lies just here: the import—for ethics and for faith—of Jewish and Christian belief in the coming fulfillment of the divine purposes for the whole of the universe.

THE CHRISTIAN FAMILY

As noted above, the Christian community clearly adopted as its basic norm for family life the life of the Jewish community—male and female created to complete the existence of each other, to bear children and to populate the earth, and to extend love and concern for each other, for relatives, and, indeed, for the larger community of faith and for all peoples.

But the larger family of faith was harder to define. It was the band of Christian believers scattered throughout the world, much on the analogy of Israel. It was a community created by God's election and love, bound together in covenant and charged to be a recognizable people in the world, doing God's will, witnessing to God's love and demands, and calling all to recognize and share in this community of the New Covenant (see especially 1 Peter 2, compared with Exod. 19:3-6). But, as noted above, this Christian community was less like a single family, descendants of a single patriarch and matriarch, than was true of the Jewish community. Jesus is reported to have said that

30

those who do the divine will are his sisters, brothers, and, indeed, his mother. The Christian larger family consists of those baptized into Christ, wherever they are to be found. What marks them as belonging to this larger family includes especially their beliefs, their style of life, and their hope for the future of God's world. Family solidarity will be harder to maintain, on such grounds, than it will be for those who can trace their lineage genealogically back to Abraham and Sarah, back to Leah and Rachel and Jacob, and whose identity is also marked by circumcision, dietary requirements, and the like.

The result is that the Christian community (Greek, *koinonia*) or fellowship or church, to a large extent, takes the place of family. The church becomes much more than the equivalent institution in Judaism, the synagogue, for it serves both as the extended family of the Christian community and as the gathering place for study, prayer, and acts of worship. What for Judaism finds embodiment in family and in synagogue, in distinct ways, is often in the Christian community found most fully and completely in church—both the local congregation in which the believer's life is centered and the larger, worldwide entity, which more and more came to be the public mode of identification of what it was that made a Christian a Christian. A Christian was, to be sure, a descendant of Jesus and the apostles and their followers; but a Christian was more concretely and really one who belonged to the family of God, represented in the local Christian congregation and also in the one worldwide church, Christ's "body."

Christian family ethics thus becomes, inevitably, both family and church ethics. What are the norms that characterize life in the Christian fellowship? Those are the very norms that obtain also for the Christian nuclear family. It is clear that there are some losses and some gains as a result of this departure from Judaism. Family life will inevitably be harder to maintain over time, since there will obviously be individuals in a nuclear family who become members of the congregation and those who do not. The New Testament makes it clear that the earliest Christian congregations often have just these features: a non-Christian husband and a Christian wife, with some children who become Christians and some who do not. Such a situation is much less characteristic of Judaism, although in those periods (including our own time) when there are many inter-marriages, families too will be divided in their religious allegiance.

The result of this experience of the Christian community as the larger family is that the ethics characteristic of the Christian family will show great variety from church to church, as the Christian community, to an extent greater than the Jewish community, will take on features and beliefs characteristic of the society within which it is located. This variety means that the elements characteristic of the Christian family worldwide will be fewer in number and harder to identify.

CHRISTIAN FAMILY PLANNING

Until recent times, contraception and efforts to stagger the birth of children within the Christian family seem to have been entirely the product of the culture within which the church was located. Only as more extended means of birth control have developed has the church faced the question of what constitutes appropriate conduct by the Christian individual and the Christian family with regard to birth control. As is well known, Roman Catholic teaching offers only limited means of interference with the processes of procreation on the part of married couples or individuals who are sexually active outside of marriage. The appearance of AIDS has contributed to a much greater readiness on the part of most churches to allow or even to encourage the use of artificial means of birth control. And for many churches, family planning and the use of birth control devices are simply accepted as an appropriate part of responsible sexual activity. The biblical command to be fruitful, to multiply, and to fill the earth (Genesis 1) is understood to call for both responsible sexual activity to continue the human community and responsible "care for the earth" so that the earth is not asked to care for a human population that it cannot be expected to sustain. The maintenance of a minimal quality of life in community comes to supplement the general affirmation of the sanctity of life in community. When families have little chance at all of supporting additional children, should they not be encouraged not to have those additional children? The issue is immensely complex, of course. We know that when the economic level of families is raised, the family will be likely to have fewer children. For this reason, population control should involve both education in techniques of contraception and major efforts to improve the living standards of individuals and communities worldwide.

CHRISTIAN SEXUAL ETHICS

Christian sexual ethics, too, is largely Jewish but includes elements from the cultures within which the Christian community came to prominence in the early centuries. For Christian sexual ethics, some of those influences were to have fateful consequences. In the Christian community, for example, the question of the goodness of the creation, so central to the faith of biblical Israel, was challenged by the widespread influence of the Greek philosopher Plato, whose thought flourished in several forms at the time of Jesus. For Plato, the creation of matter, of the material universe, could not have been done by God directly, for the creation lacks perfection and is constantly involved in change and decay. In some Christian circles, the Bible's insistence upon the goodness of the whole of creation was maintained, but only for the "original" creation, that known by Adam and Eve prior to their sin. With the coming of sin came also death—for all. The whole of human history thus came to be viewed by many Christians as so damaged and marred by human sin that it was simply a "body of death," as Paul called it once (Rom. 7:24).[3]

The Christian doctrine of original sin, rightly understood, does not at all deny the goodness of God's creation. Human sin can and should be understood to have "touched" the whole of God's good creation, to have distorted and damaged all features of life on God's earth. But the essential goodness of God's creation remains intact, just as God's essential purposes for the whole of creation remain intact. When the Christian doctrine of original sin is understood to refer to the inevitable (or almost inevitable) consequences of the life lived out by frail and anxious human beings on God's good earth, then the doctrine of the goodness of the creation remains intact.

3. This idea is shared in some Jewish circles; see, for example, the first-century C.E. book titled Second Esdras or Fourth Ezra, found in some early Christian Bibles and regularly included today in editions of the Apocrypha, also called the Deutero-canonical writings.

Human sin, in this view, comes about as human beings, created in the image of God, attempt to fulfill their place in God's world, sharing the joys of life with God and also the responsibility of caring for God's good earth. As they do so, they are inevitably (or almost inevitably) driven either to try to improve upon God's creation or to neglect their responsibilities. What prompts them to do such fateful things? Their very freedom under God's overall guidance of the universe makes such action possible, and the very conditions of human temporal life make such an outcome virtually certain. Sometimes the cardinal sin is viewed as pride or self-love, the turning in upon itself of the self. It is better thought of, perhaps, as, at its heart, an anxious desire both to please God and to please oneself and those whom one most loves. Anxiety is not sin, but it sets the stage for sin.

The problem for sexual ethics in all this lies in two features of a Christian understanding of sin that have a long history in the Christian community. Both of these are immensely harmful, and they do in fact go together, to some extent.

The first distortion of the Christian understanding of original sin, which has caused massive damage in the course of the history of the church, is to understand that this original sin of the first human pair was passed along to the next generations, not socially, as one generation naturally passes along its thought and its practices to the next generation, but in the very act of procreation, the sexual act. When the sexual act is understood to have such a byproduct, such consequences, then sexuality itself is virtually sure to be treated as somehow tainted by human sin in a special way, and thus somehow partaking of sin *every time persons come together sexually.*

Since human sexuality involves the sharing of life in the most intimate of ways, it also involves enormous human vulnerability and the capacity for all kinds of mistreatment. It is not surprising, then, that the second feature of Christian social ethics should have developed: *making sexual attraction and engagement the very cause of the first sin.* In this view, it is Eve the seductress who takes advantage of her husband, who cannot resist her blandishments. The woman thus becomes the first tempter, despite the clear biblical pictures: The woman (along with her husband, who is with her all the time [see Gen. 3:6]), engages in debate with the tempter, sees the logic of not letting good food go unused, is drawn by the beauty of the tree and

34

its fruit, and is especially captivated by the prospect of securing wisdom and greater understanding. The first sin, according to the Bible, engages all of the gifts and resources of the first human pair. Fatefully, these gifts and resources are put to use in an act of betrayal of the trust that has marked the life of the first human pair with God. This betrayal of trust, this departure from loyal love, produces the first sin. In each life and in each generation the consequences of this first betrayal of trust are passed along socially and culturally. These consequences provide the moral context in which all human acts take place. In that context, the first betrayal is ever so likely to be repeated. For the Christian, it is God's act in Jesus as Messiah and Savior that breaks that dreary context and offers fresh opportunities for faithfulness and obedience and for taking up one's life *now* in the Age to Come. That act of God in Jesus is affirmed in the Christian community and continues to be effectual there.

The Christian understanding of human sin does, of course, involve sexuality, to the extent that one generation does, humanly speaking, produce the next generation through the act of procreation. But all too often Christians have treated sexuality as part of a "fallen" creation and therefore no longer a good gift of God. Even worse, many Christians have seen in the sexual act a particular example of human temptation to sin, if not actual sin itself.

Small wonder, then, that in those communities around the Mediterranean world in which the Christian community took root there would have been a temptation to view the physical world and its hold upon the soul with suspicion and to consider Christian salvation as a means of escape from the world in order to be with God. In the religious outlook called Gnosticism, the soul was considered to have been *flung* into earthly existence, from which it could escape by means of the knowledge and the practices offered by Gnostic communities. Otherworldly Christianity could easily be captivated by this Gnostic outlook.

But over and again in the history of the Christian community the Jewish understanding of the goodness of the creation, which is also a Christian understanding, has come to the aid of a Christian community that was prone to take an alternative view.

When the creation is understood as God's good creation, badly scarred and twisted and damaged as a result of human sin, human sexuality must be viewed as the good gift of a good God. The Bible makes that very clear, especially in texts from the Hebrew Scriptures. In the Hebrew Bible, sex is both a means of procreation and peopling the earth and also a divine gift for human beings to enjoy. The Song of Songs is all about human sexual delight, with not a reference to children. The aged Sarah can speak of having fun with her husband when a child is being promised (Gen. 18:12). As Rabbi Falk has pointed out, sexual pleasure is a part of the goodness of life under God. With all the stress upon the importance of children, especially sons, in biblical texts, both the Hebrew Bible and the New Testament insist that there is no connection as such between sexuality and sin; on the contrary, sexual pleasure is God's good gift.

Sexual imagery is even applied to God in the Bible, although it is for the sake of underscoring the love with which God loves the people of the covenant. Essentially, God is beyond the distinction of male and female, even though God can be referred to with the use of both male and female imagery, including sexual imagery. Apparently, this break with ancient Near Eastern religious practices of depicting the gods as sharing sexual longing, bearing divine children, and engaging in sexual misconduct was due largely to the stress upon the oneness of God, though it is a oneness in plurality. In Judaism as well as in Christianity, God is not conceived of as living in isolation. God is surrounded by a host of those who do the divine bidding, and God has intimate partnership with Wisdom, with Torah (God's instruction and guidance), with Word and Spirit. In early Christian thought the doctrine of the divine Trinity, three "persons" in one "substance" or "nature," seeks to affirm the unity of God that is disclosed in the formula God, Son, and Holy Spirit. Even so, Christian faith always holds, with Judaism, to the divine oneness, which means that the "family" of God will be the human family, and in particular the covenant family of those who have entrusted their all to the deity.

Jesus' teaching on sexuality seems thoroughly Jewish, although it is clearly marked by the affirmation of the nearness of the Age to Come. He does not marry, but he certainly rejoices in the life of those who have married. Many parables have to do with the joys of bride and bridegroom, and the first miracle recorded (John 2) shows Jesus providing for additional wine at a marriage feast in Cana. Jesus is very strict in his teaching on divorce, but ready to spend time with women charged with sexual misconduct. Paul speaks of Jesus as having shared fully the trials and the joys of life, including temptation to sin, while remaining without sin (see 2 Cor. 5:21).

Paul's attitude toward sex is more guarded. He can wish that the Corinthians were all unmarried, as he is, but he grants that marriage is better than for one to burn with sexual passion. Here, too, however, Paul points toward the shortness of the time before the consummation of God's purpose. He clearly insists (1 Corinthians 7) that some are called to one form of sexual life and others to another. Whether married or unmarried, one is to receive the sexual gift as God's good gift and employ the gift responsibly.

The New Testament has three texts that clearly prohibit sexual relations between persons of the same sex: Romans 1:26-27; 1 Corinthians 6:9; and 1 Timothy 1:10. These passages, along with two from the Hebrew Scriptures (Lev. 18:22; 20:13) are the only direct prohibitions of homosexual practice in the Bible. No texts address the question of homosexual orientation. Homosexual rape is envisaged in the story of Lot's protection of the angels who visit him in Sodom (Genesis 19) and in the account of the Levite who gains shelter in the city of Gibeah but does not protect his concubine from the criminal assault of the men of the town (Judges 19). The New Testament texts probably have in view primarily the use of children by adults for sexual gratification, a practice known to be widespread in the Greek and Roman worlds of the time.

The Christian norm for all sexual behavior, which is also clearly a Jewish norm, is sexual engagement that enriches and enhances life in community rather than damaging that life. The sexual act is a giving and a receiving of pleasure, as God intended that it be. Exploitative or cruel or violent sexual acts damage life in community and have no place in Christian life, of course. As noted above, some Christians believe that any artificial means of preventing the birth of children is forbidden, because of the sanctity of life itself. But no Christian should consider the sharing of life and the enjoyment of life sexually to be inappropriate or wrong, so long as the sharing is intended to enhance life in community.

The use of the phrase "in community" is, of course, critical. Individuals who engage in sexual activity simply for their own

pleasure and with no thought of the sexual partner or the consequences of that behavior will almost surely fall under criticism by
the Christian community. The joining of two persons sexually is, as
both Genesis and Paul say (Gen. 2:2-24; 1 Cor. 6:16), the creation of
a new unity. One may not intend that this be so; the sex may be
treated as a casual act. But is it ever just a casual act? Does not a new
bond get created in the very act itself—if the act is a human act at
all?

No doubt, individuals can and do survive sexual acts that do not
measure up to this Christian understanding. But a Christian understanding of sexuality would identify at least the following three
features: (1) It is intended to give pleasure to both partners; (2) it is
not exploitative but rather aims at enhancing life in community; and
(3) it expresses a commitment to the partner that is intended to be
lifelong.

Christians need to face the question of whether sexual acts between persons of the same sex that meet the above three criteria can
be affirmed, or at least recognized as acceptable even if not fully
affirmed. Clearly, persons with an orientation to homosexuality are
not to be discriminated against by anyone, since homosexuality
seems largely to be a part of the makeup of persons at birth. Since
the sexual dimensions of human existence are of such profound
weight and mystery, it is not surprising that we should be disturbed
or offended when persons engage in forms of behavior that we take
not to follow the norms. Moreover, since a few biblical texts clearly
reject homosexual behavior, some Christians will insist that no forms
of sexual activity between persons of the same sex can be acceptable
Christian conduct.

In my view, all Christians need to commit themselves to the
criteria of wholesome sexual activity listed above. I see no reasons
in principle why persons of the same sex cannot accept and follow
those guidelines. Indeed, I know gay and lesbian couples who, so
far as I can see, do follow the norms.

One additional point might be appropriate. Marriage, family life,
and human sexuality all have in view the future, the next generation.
The command to be fruitful, to multiply, and to fill the earth should
never be taken lightly by any follower of the biblical heritage. Does
that not mean that every human being has a commitment under God

to children, to members of the next generation? If the answer is yes, then that should suggest that every individual, every heterosexual and homosexual couple without children, just as much as families with children, should make a formal commitment to children. There are enough children in the world who have no parents or children with parents who cannot adequately care for them to supply the needs of childless individuals and couples.

SUGGESTED READING

Childress, James F., and John Macquarrie, eds. *The Westminster Dictionary of Christian Ethics*. Rev. ed. Philadelphia: Westminster, 1986.

Culbertson, Philip F. *New Adam: The Future of Male Spirituality*. Maryknoll, N.Y.: Orbis, 1992.

Harrelson, Walter. *The Ten Commandments and Human Rights*. Philadelphia: Fortress, 1980.

Nelson, James. *Embodiment: An Approach to Sexuality and Christian Theology*. Minneapolis: Augsburg, 1978.

Smith, Wallace Charles. *The Church in the Life of the Black Family*. Valley Forge, Pa.: Judson, 1986.

CHAPTER TWO

RELIGIOUS LIBERTY

A JEWISH OUTLOOK

Hanukkah is the Jewish holiday that celebrates the first victory for religious liberty in the history of humankind. It commemorates the military triumph of the Maccabean army over the Syrian forces in 165 B.C.E., as described in the books of the Maccabees in the Apocrypha. The Judeans were then able to reclaim their Temple in Jerusalem, cleanse it, remove the statue of the Syrian despot Antiochus IV, who had required that all Jews bow before his image on entering the Temple gates. Then they were able to resume their worship of the One God. The word *Hanukkah* means "dedication," and the holiday emphasizes the privilege of free men and women to worship as our consciences dictate. Pope Pius XII once made this statement: "Had there been no Hanukkah, there could be no Christmas." He underscored the fact that without this victory for religious liberty, freedom to worship the One God would possibly have been lost for Jews, Christians, and Muslims for all time.

Jewish history is replete with accounts of oppression and persecution when a government enforced the observance of a state religion on its entire citizenry, completely rejecting the right of members of minority religions to follow dictates of their consciences. The second instance of this occurred early in the fourth century of the common era when Constantine declared Christianity to be the official religion of the Roman Empire. At the same time, he prohibited adherents of Judaism, Hellenism, and other religions within the empire to proselytize. In order to enforce this prohibition, Constantine forbade Jews to have any non-Jews working in their homes. He limited Jewish Sabbath and holiday observances. Jews essentially had to go underground in their religious activity.

The most tragic example of religious tyranny occurred in the Spanish Inquisition during the latter years of the fifteenth century. Jews were required either to convert to Catholicism or to flee the land. Some chose to live as Marranos (outwardly Christian but remaining Jews in secret); but when discovered by the Inquisitors, they were burned on fiery platforms.

In modern history, the same pattern of persecution of a minority religion was seen in tsarist Russia. Entire Jewish communities were massacred for no other reason than the assertion of control over religious practice by the Russian Orthodox Church, maintaining its power through close ties with the tsarist regime. Throughout Jewish history, in almost every nation on earth, in one era or another, Jews have been oppressed or exiled when a majority religion has been recognized by the government as the official religion of the land. Through the combined power of the government officials and the religious leaders, no minority religion was tolerated. These lessons from history have made most Jews deeply committed to the doctrine of separation of church and state.

Even in the New World, religious liberty was not easily achieved. Many of the thirteen North American colonies were established by religious bodies seeking to escape persecution in the old world. They were interested, however, only in establishing their own freedom without concern for the liberties of persons of other faiths living in their midst. A typical example of this was found in the Massachusetts Bay Colony, where refusal to allow a religious minority to follow the dictates of conscience prompted Roger Williams and his followers to leave and found their own colony in Rhode Island. These Baptists were the first religious group to establish freedom for all faiths in their colony.

In New Amsterdam the governor, Peter Stuyvesant, sought to refuse admission to the colony for some twenty-seven Jews who had fled the long arm of the Inquisition, which had reached them in Brazil in 1654. When New Amsterdam's parent organization, the West Indies Company of the Netherlands, overruled Stuyvesant, the Jews were allowed to settle in New Amsterdam, though not as equal citizens. The governor ruled that instead of taking their regular turns in guard duty, the Jews would be required to pay a special tax to have citizens of the colony serve in their stead. Only after a lengthy court battle was this discriminatory law removed from the colony's statutes. The last discriminatory laws against Jews were not removed from some state statutes until the middle of the nineteenth century.

For all of these reasons, most American Jews have sought zealously to safeguard Article VI of the Constitution: "No religious test shall ever be required as a qualification to any office or public trust under the United States"; and especially the First Amendment to the Constitution: "Congress shall make no law respecting an establishment of religion or prohibiting the free exercise thereof." These laws have been challenged in many areas of school and community activity, and the interpretations of the law in state and federal courts have varied from very narrow to broad decisions on specific issues.

Robert L. Maddox, in his book *Separation of Church and State: Guarantor of Religious Freedom,* observes that slowly but surely religious liberties are slipping into oblivion. There are polls that show an alarmingly increasing deterioration of support for religious liberties, and their main governmental guarantee: the separation of church and state. Maddox warns: "We must see, as never before, that liberty of conscience exists as the foundation on which all other freedoms build. If the government or charismatic religious leadership gain the power to coerce or to manipulate religious belief, and to intimidate practices, 'all' our 'freedoms' will crumble!"[1]

The area in which Jews have been most concerned with maintenance of separation of church and state has been in the public schools. With the exception of some Orthodox Jews, the American Jewish community has vigorously opposed prayer in classrooms, prayer at athletic events and at graduation ceremonies, school-sponsored baccalaureate services, Bible reading, released time for religious instruction in public schools, and placing of religious symbols on school or other public property. Led by its national civic defense organizations—the National Jewish Community Relations Advisory Council, the Anti-Defamation League, the American Jewish Committee, and the American Jewish Congress—American Jews have joined like-minded organizations in the Christian and the secular communities in legal challenges to any infringements on separation of church and state within the public schools.

The essential doctrine by which the United States Supreme Court

---

1. R. L. Maddox, *Separation of Church and State* (New York: Crossroad, 1987) 3.

refused to allow these various religious activities in the schools was enunciated in the majority decision in *Everson v. Board of Education* (1947):

> The establishment of the religion clause of the First Amendment means at least this: neither a state nor the federal government can set up a church. Neither can pass laws that aid one religion, aid all religions, or prefer one religion over another. Neither can force nor influence a person to go to or remain away from church against his will or force him to profess a belief or disbelief in any religion. No person can be punished for entertaining or professing religious beliefs or disbeliefs, for church attendance or nonattendance. No tax in any amount, large or small, can be levied to support any religious activities or institutions, whatever they may be called, or whatever form they may adopt to teach or practice religion. Neither a state nor the federal government can, openly or secretly, participate in the affairs of any religious organization or groups and vice versa. In the words of Jefferson, the clause against establishment of religion by law was intended to erect a wall of separation between church and state.[2]

In the decade of the 1990s, strenuous efforts have been launched by the Religious Right to reverse or eliminate the patterns of separation of church and state in the public schools. Some moderates in both the Jewish and the Christian communities have urged consideration of some compromise proposals:

1. *Silent meditation at the beginning of the school day.* Could this allow time for prayer without requiring that a child pray at a specified time and without infringing on any individual's rights or beliefs, or would this simply be the first crack in the wall of separation, leading to further demands for prayer in the classroom?

2. *Teaching the Bible as literature.* Is it possible to teach the Bible as literature without interpreting many passages from a particular religious perspective?

3. *Teaching about religions.* It could be very helpful to explain the history and the basic cultural traditions of all faiths to promote understanding of and respect for the variety of religious experiences children from diverse backgrounds enjoy. This is especially impor-

---

2. Cited in A. Vorspan and D. Saperstein, *Tough Choices* (New York: UAHC Press, 1992) 70-71.

tant with the large influx of people whose religious heritages are Islamic, Buddhist, and Hindu. Is it possible to find teachers qualified to teach about religions in an objective, nontheological approach?

4. *Character education, based on the moral truths and ethical principles that all religions share.* Should this be a separate course, or is character education something that is taught by example and by the way in which interpersonal relationships are handled in day-by-day experiences in the classroom?

5. *Joint holiday celebrations, such as Christmas-Hanukkah parties.* Can such celebrations be held without including specific religious music, stories, and symbols?

6. *General, all-inclusive prayers at graduation exercises or other school events.* Can all religious groups pray without including specific theological phrases, such as "in Christ's name"? How do we satisfy agnostics or atheists who do not believe in prayer?

One compromise was effected through the 1994 Equal Access Legislation. It sought to provide the right for purely voluntary student religious groups, such as Bible clubs, to meet on public school premises as do other special-interest clubs. The groups had to be student-initiated, and guest speakers could be invited, but not with regularity. As might be expected, this compromise has brought many abuses, especially by overzealous evangelical leaders. This has caused great concern on the part of Jewish parents.

The other major concern with regard to separation of church and state in education is the growing pressure to use federal funds for support of various activities and programs in parochial schools. The fear, of course, is that public schools, already so terribly under-funded, would be in even more difficult financial straits if their revenues were shared with parochial and private schools. Other threats to the stability of public education funds have been support from some quarters, including former President Bush, for "educational choice"—that is, allowing parents to choose between public and private schools, providing government funds to the school selected through vouchers or tax credits. Although the proponents of such plans argue that this is not support of private schools with government funds, since the payments go to the parents, the end result is provision of public funds to support private and parochial schools.

Vorspan and Saperstein report in *Tough Choices* that "in recent years, the Jewish community has been split on the key issue of federal aid to parochial schools. The Orthodox community, which maintains a large and growing system of day schools, believes that federal aid to religious schools is not a violation of separation of church and state. Orthodox leaders have argued that the United States government must take responsibility for the education of every American child, no matter what kind of school he or she may attend. Many Jewish groups—including the Conservative and Reform movements, each of which has in the past decades begun its own day school systems—continue to believe that, while a person has every right to send a child to a nonpublic school that teaches religious dogma, no one has the right to ask the government to pay for it."[3]

In 1837, Massachusetts set up the first board of education in America, electing Horace Mann its secretary. Mann insisted that education have a strong moral tone while avoiding sectarian, religious instruction. He and others like him who pioneered in public education had a place for the Bible in their schools, but religious teachings were to be generic, general in approach. No church could ever be allowed to control the schools. Mann could hold against sectarian religious instruction, while accommodating generic religion, because almost everyone in Massachusetts agreed on the broad religious concepts. Along with this nonsectarian instruction, the idea of not levying tax money for sectarian schools also had wide acceptance. By 1855, Massachusetts had a provision forbidding the state from giving any funding to sectarian schools.[4]

In recent times, the American Jewish community has had to face crucial questions regarding its relationship to the public schools. With public education deteriorating in many communities throughout the country, due primarily to inadequate funding, the move toward Jewish day schools has increased significantly. Not only has the Orthodox Jewish community expanded its day school system, but the Conservative and Reform movements have done so as well. Reform Judaism, which once vigorously opposed religious day schools, now has a growing number of those schools in its congre-

3. See ibid., 75.
4. Maddox, *Separation of Church and State*, 101-2.

gations. If they believe that the public schools are the cornerstone of American democracy, and if they believe that the fight for the preservation of separation of church and state begins in public schools, then how can Reform Jews join the large numbers of middle and upper middle-class families in withdrawing their children from public schools to enter private sectarian and secular schools?

The Union of American Hebrew Congregations confronted this dilemma at its 1985 biennial convention. Should it encourage full-time Reform Jewish day schools, and thus virtually abandon, or at least weaken, their support of the public school system, in order to place new emphasis on intensifying Jewish education? The delegates to the convention sought to reach a compromise in a resolution that held that its commitment to public schools should not preclude its support for legitimate efforts to strengthen Jewish education through the option of day schools. Such support, however, was predicated on two conditions: first, that synagogues undertake efforts to strengthen the public schools in their communities and, second, that the movement reaffirm its commitment to separation of church and state, including opposition to federal aid to full-time religious education. Needless to say, Jewish congregations and communities that are supporting day schools have been able to do little to assist the public schools in their communities.[5]

Closely related to the problems created by support of day schools versus public schools, and the increasing pressure for various kinds of federal aid for day schools, has been the matter of federal support for pre-school child care. In 1990, Congress passed a comprehensive child-care bill, which initially had the enthusiastic support of the Reform Jewish movement. The bill provided that funds could go to churches and synagogues conducting child-care programs, as long as those programs were nonsectarian and did not discriminate against pupils and employees on the basis of religion. At the last minute, however, an amendment was added to strike the limitation allowing for federal support for overtly sectarian child-care programs. Although the UAHC decided to oppose the bill with that amendment, the bill passed. Those who maintain that this is a serious violation of separation of church and state now await a test case that will eventually wind up in the U.S. Supreme Court.

5. Vorspan and Saperstein, *Tough Choices*, 21-22.

Issues of separation of church and state do not revolve solely around matters of public education and child care. One of the most important Supreme Court decisions involving church-state relationships was the 1971 case of *Lemon v. Kurtzman*. Under the so-called "Lemon test," to be constitutional a law or other act of government (1) must have a secular purpose; (2) must not have a primary effect that either advances or inhibits religion; and (3) must not foster "excessive entanglement" between religion and government. Despite this strong and clear statement that enforces the wall of separation, subsequent court rulings on matters of religious symbols in public buildings and on public property have been, to say the least, confusing.

In 1985, the Supreme Court ruled that the city of Pawtucket, Rhode Island, could use state funds to pay for its nativity scene, even on private property. Then in 1989, in the case of *County of Allegheny v. the American Civil Liberties Union*, the Court decided that a crèche standing in a courthouse lobby was a religious symbol inappropriate for display on public property. At the same time, however, the Court upheld the constitutionality of a menorah on display on the plaza outside of the county courthouse. The Court based this latter ruling of the menorah as a neutral religious symbol on the fact that it stood next to a Christmas tree.

Reform Jewish organizations, along with some of the secular Jewish organizations, have opposed the concept that a menorah can, under any circumstances, lose its Jewish religious significance. These groups have, therefore, consistently opposed the Lubavitch chasidic community in its efforts to place large menorahs in public parks to "balance" the nativity scenes annually displayed in those parks. Those opposed to the menorahs on public property maintain that this can seriously undermine the concept of separation of church and state.

Separation of church and state was dealt a severe blow when, in 1990, the Supreme Court rendered a decision in the case of *Employment Division of Oregon v. Smith*. This case dealt with the right of Native Americans to use peyote in religious ceremonies. Peyote is a colorless, alcoholic liquor made from the fermented juices of various agave plants. It has been used in religious ceremonies for centuries by Mexican Indians for its hallucinogenic effects. In the decision by the majority of the Supreme Court justices, denying the Native Americans the right to use peyote in their religious ceremonies, they seriously weakened the protection of freedom of religion in the United States. In writing the majority decision, Justice Antonin Scalia stated that "the traditional protection of religious freedom—the 'compelling state interest' test is a 'luxury' that America can no longer afford."[6]

The far-reaching effects of this decision are a grave concern for Jews. Based on this decision, the courts can ban the use of sacramental wine by children for Sabbath and holy day observances. It may also be the basis for denying prisoners, Jewish or Muslim, the right not to be served pork in violation of their religious practices.

If the Supreme Court will no longer serve as the guarantor of our basic religious rights, it will be necessary to turn to Congress to preserve these rights. Recently, Congress has been requested to consider the Religious Restoration Act (RRA), which would restore the "compelling state interest" test. All of this serves notice that we must be increasingly vigilant in order to ensure that basic religious freedom remains a cornerstone of American democracy.[7]

Unfortunately, the Jewish community in the United States is no longer united in matters of separation of church and state. Orthodox Jews have aligned themselves with some Christian fundamentalists in seeking public funds for day schools and in permitting prayer and Bible reading in classrooms and at other school functions. For many Reform, Conservative, and secular Jews the gravest concerns focus on the areas in which the Religious Right has called for a "religious war" to control the culture of America. Many of the far-right groups are mobilizing to demand of city and state governments concessions to religious groups, which openly breaches the wall of separation of church and state.

Obviously Jews are not the only group affected by the widening breach in the wall of separation. Every religious minority in America—Muslims, Hindus, Buddhists, Native Americans, and others—must unite in facing our common concerns. Certainly it is important, too, for the liberal Christian community to be sensitive to these concerns and to join in our efforts to preserve religious liberty in the

6. Ibid., 66.
7. See ibid., 66-67.

United States, as was set forth in our Constitution and our Bill of Rights.

SUGGESTED READING

Maddox, R. L. *Separation of Church and State.* New York: Crossroad, 1987.
Pfeiffer, L. *Church State and Freedom.* Boston: Beacon Press, 1967.
———. *Creeds in Competition.* New York: Harper and Bros., 1958.
Saperstein, D. *The Challenge of the Religious Right: A Jewish Response.* Washington, D.C.: Commission on Social Action of Reform Judaism.
Vorspan, A. *Great Jewish Debates and Dilemmas.* New York: Union of American Hebrew Congregations, 1980.
Vorspan, A., and D. Saperstein. *Tough Choices.* New York: UAHC Press, 1992.

RELIGIOUS LIBERTY

A CHRISTIAN OUTLOOK

For the Christian community, religious liberty is both a wise provision of American democracy and a demand of faith. The early Christians found themselves forbidden by the civil authorities from the practice of their religion (Acts 5), and they had no choice but to declare, "We must obey God rather than mortals." The two features of religious liberty go hand in hand, for the religious liberty that the Christian community must insist upon theologically is also a liberty that the community of faith desires for all individuals and groups. Both Judaism and Christianity have reasons of faith for insisting upon religious liberty, and both have experience that shows the wisdom of our founding ancestors who provided in the Bill of Rights the twofold demands of the First Amendment: (1) Congress is not to give preference by law to any particular religion, and (2) it is not to act in any way that would abridge the free exercise of religion by any citizen. No establishment of religion and also no impediment to the practice of religion—those are the two pillars of religious liberty in American political life.

Until recently, the Christian community in the United States has affirmed both of these pillars, both for religious and for nonreligious reasons. In recent times, as Rabbi Falk has noted, there are challenges to both of these pillars. In their anxiety about the decline of morals and standards of public and private conduct, many Christians have come to believe that it is appropriate to insist that the United States is, in principle, a Christian country and that something like a Christian establishment is only right and proper. And more positively, many Christians see in the "free exercise" clause sufficient justification for pressing to have prayer in the public schools and forms of indirect support for religion from the state. To be denied opportunity for officially sanctioned prayer in the public schools is felt by some to be a denial of the right to exercise one's religion freely, and not to be able to use tax monies in support of one's religious school system is deemed a denial of the same right.

What is the ground, *theologically*, for the Christian insistence that "we must obey God and not mortals"? The grounding is, as one might expect, found in the Jewish Scriptures and is reaffirmed by the Christian community.

THE BIBLICAL BASIS FOR RELIGIOUS LIBERTY

Hypothetically, Judaism, Christianity, and Islam might be thought to look for the day when there is no distinction between the religious community and the secular state. In such a situation, there would be no need for religious liberty, for all the citizens would belong to the religious community and would be bound by its religious insights and demands. But in actuality, there never has been such a Jewish or Christian or Muslim commonwealth. Some texts in the Hebrew Scriptures suggest that the intended purpose of the God of Israel was for the people to enter the land of Canaan, root out every human being who would not convert to the religion of Israel, and strictly enforce the demands of the God of Israel upon all citizens. In that situation, God alone is king in the land, and leadership is chosen by the divine Spirit. Religious freedom would no longer be needed or desired, for all would be worshiping God as God had purposed, and there would be no dissenters or nonbelievers.

The Bible itself indicates that Israel never undertook to destroy all the nonbelievers. Over and over again, as Rabbi Falk has shown, other views prevailed, and Israel developed its own religious life in the midst of those who worshiped the deities of the land of Canaan or of some other locality (see Joshua 24 for a programmatic text that indicates how Israel actually settled the land of Canaan, understanding that God was giving the land to Israel but not insisting that nonbelievers be destroyed). And with the coming of kingship to Israel at the end of the eleventh century B.C.E., the community explicitly recognized that the demands of the covenant faith were not in

51

fact to be fully embodied in the state, even though the selection of Israel's first three kings (Saul, David, and Solomon) was understood to have been done through agents designated by God. A Jewish commonwealth was indeed envisaged by the prophets, but the forcing of religious demands or the royal meddling in the conduct of religion could be fatal.

What we see is, for practical purposes, a separation of "church" and "state" already in the time of the early Israelite monarchy. David can become the beloved king whom people will follow with almost fanatical devotion, but David is not above or beyond the law of God. The prophet Nathan condemns his colleague and friend for having taken the wife of another man and for having that man murdered (see 2 Samuel 11–12). And at a later time, the prophet Amos can roundly denounce the royal priest Amaziah at the northern Israelite shrine of Bethel when this priest insists that prophets of God must never say anything too critical of the king and the other leaders of the state.

For the prophet Amos, even the "establishment" of a religion not based on justice and fairness for all citizens must be attacked and condemned: "Come to Bethel, and transgress!" The more one worships at the royal shrines appointed to show how religious this unjust state has become, the more one transgresses God's law. Giving some kind of divine sanction or status to what we call a "secular" state is already called into question by the prophet Amos in the middle of the eighth century B.C.E.

Even so, it must be acknowledged that the Christian community has been favored, over and again, by governments, from the time of the Roman Emperor Constantine to the twentieth century.[1] Christianity still has a kind of "established" status in a number of secular states, but the time has long passed when religious leaders in such states can in fact direct the course of governmental policy. Note, for example, the fact that the sale of contraceptives and the possibility of legal abortions are both state policy in Italy, despite the strong objections of the Vatican and of Christian leaders within Italy.

The ground for religious liberty lies in the covenant faith of Israel

---

1. Constantine did not establish Christianity as the religion of the empire; his son Constantius did that. But Constantine did give legitimacy to Christianity throughout the empire, and his own conversion to Christianity and his public leadership of Christian gatherings gave immense standing and prestige to the Christian community.

and of the Christian community, as we noted above. It lies particularly in the Israelite recognition that the holy God is the only absolute authority over human beings created in the divine image. The exclusive claims of the God of the covenant require that the state not constrain the religious liberty of the people of the covenant. The laws of a given land are not, or not fully, the laws of God. The honor to be conferred upon political and cultural leaders does not partake of the divine, for God alone is God. This bold and revolutionary separation between the realm of the divine and the human is the cornerstone of religious liberty for those religious communities that claim the Hebrew Scriptures as authoritative.

Over and over again in the Hebrew Bible this distinction is underscored. The prophet Isaiah, a great friend and supporter of the kings of Judah and a great champion of the importance of the capital city, Jerusalem, can still speak of the faithful city that has become utterly corrupt, of judges and leaders who turn their backs on justice. The prophet then offers pictures of a true and righteous Jerusalem that God will create, to the shame and devastation of the current city. And the prophets Micah and Jeremiah can even affirm that God intends the utter destruction of this capital town, the beloved city conquered and built up by King David and promised as the seat of government for a kingship that will endure forever (2 Samuel 7; see also Jeremiah 26; Mic. 3:12).

Jesus comes with a message for the "lost sheep of the house of Israel," a message that also includes warnings against Jerusalem for its faithlessness and against religious authorities who get in the way of God's just demands and do not do their part in the fulfilling of God's promises for Israel and for the nations of earth. Once again, it is the exclusive claim of the One God that lies behind the relativizing of all other authorities and brings the demand for religious liberty. Those who would compel the early Christians to worship the deities of the Roman state must be resisted, for there is one God only, known most intimately and personally in the Messiah Jesus, God's beloved Son, by the power of the Holy Spirit.

At the same time, just as one must not be compelled to worship some other deity, so also one must not be compelled to worship the triune God of Christian faith. That has been a harder lesson for the Christian community to learn through the centuries. If we have the truth of life, the revelation that is ultimate for all peoples and for all time, why should we not impose it upon others? The answer is clear: Precisely because God alone is ultimate, God alone can impose that ultimate truth. Individuals who worship the One God of Jewish and Christian faith are called to recognize that the initiative for such an exclusive demand always lies with God. When the political and religious authorities are about to put Jeremiah to death for his public stand among them, he can only say, "It is truly God who has sent me," and then leave his life in their hands, warning them that if they take his life, they take the life of an innocent person, not a traitor (Jeremiah 26). Jeremiah does not organize a bloodbath to impose his understanding of God upon the society. The effort of King Jehu to do that in Israel in the ninth century B.C.E. ended in disaster and frightful cost of human life (2 Kings 9–11). Jeremiah lives out his life among fellow citizens, most of whom never come to his religious viewpoint. But they are his colleagues and friends, and on many occasions they come to his rescue when his life is about to be taken.

Similarly, Jesus' own witness among the Jewish people of his day is the farthest thing from an effort to impose his understandings upon all who hear him. Like the prophets before him, he bears his testimony, does so forcefully, skillfully, insistently, and is ready to pay with his life for the truth of that testimony. The biblical evidence makes it clear that one can proclaim the religious understanding that in faith one knows to be the truth of life, but in a way that does not demand that hearers assent to that truth.

We see, then, that there is solid grounding in the Scriptures for the Jewish and Christian understandings of religious liberty. A wholesome and just political entity will allow for the practice of religion without hindrance, so long as that practice is not a clear and direct threat to the health and the very life of those who practice it. Borderline cases will test the ability of the state to know when religious practices become life threatening and must be interfered with (the practice of snake handling, for example, or the refusal to permit one's children to have blood transfusions even in the face of the child's imminent death). Since Jews and Christians know that God and God alone has ultimate authority over their lives, they must insist that interference with the free exercise of their faith would be an assault upon God's freedom to claim them and demand their full allegiance. And if that is true of them, how can they then not protect the freedom of all to practice their religious faith as they have come to understand that faith? If the state cannot tell *us* how to worship, is it tolerable for the state to tell any citizen how to worship?

THE "CHRISTIAN" STATE

In the history of Christianity, there have been many instances in which the Christian community has secured control of the government and has, for a time, imposed Christianity upon all citizens. We have seen that there was a similar movement in ancient Israel that aimed in the same direction.[2] The forced conversion of whole tribes and peoples is a well-known part of European and North and South American history, and the expulsion of the Jews from European lands is another clear example of such intolerance in the name of Christian faith. Eventually, however, forms of religious establishment have been worked out that offer protection of those who do not share the outlook of the established body. And in the modern state of Israel, Orthodox Judaism is the established religion with constitutional provisions designed to protect the rights of non-Jewish religions. The Orthodox "establishment" in Israel is being urged to make concessions in order to ensure religious liberty for the non-Orthodox Jewish religious community as well. Many Jews worldwide chafe under the present arrangement. For them, the important thing is that there be a state with a majority of Jewish citizens, regardless of their religious or secular preference, so that Israel can remain a homeland or a potential homeland for all Jews, as well as a sign of security for Jews in the world, given the Holocaust. The state of Israel is one powerful way of saying, "Never again!"

The establishment of a given religion in various lands has proved to be quite problematic over the years. Some gains are evident: It has been possible, for example, for the public schools of "establishment" lands to provide a curriculum in Bible and religion that is often quite

2. The so-called Deuteronomistic History is often seen to have espoused the harsh view reflected in such texts as Exodus 23 and 33 and Joshua 11. The irony is that the same Deuteronomistic literature that contains these texts also contains their opposite, revealing a strong commitment to protect the rights of the stranger, the member of the minority.

objective and provides a much needed presentation of the religious heritage for the community, both the religious and the secular communities. The provision of state funds secured through taxation has enabled ministries of education to provide for theological education for the clergy at the universities and otherwise to ensure capable instruction in the religious heritage of the citizenry.

Critics of the establishment of religion point out, however, that actual participation in religious worship and the public practice of one's faith often seem to decline in lands where a particular religion has state support. The founders of the United States, and other nations as well, have sought to leave the teaching and the practice of religious faith to the religious bodies themselves, placing no barrier in their way as they do so, but also not favoring any particular religion over another.

THE RELIGIOUS RIGHT

As we noted above, many Christians today are determined to see the United States government and the local governments of the states and municipalities give greater place to the teaching and the practice of Christianity than is now held to be allowable by law and judicial interpretation. The argument is that the states and the courts today are not maintaining neutrality but are actually favoring what is called the "religion" of secular humanism. Many of us believe that this is a mistaken understanding of secular humanism, although we would not for a moment deny that there are many secular voices in public life, in our schools, and in our judicial system as well, voices that have no particular interest in or regard for religion in any of its forms.

Many of us also believe that it is wise for the religious communities to work very diligently to provide public instruction in religion in our state and private colleges and universities and to offer on a strictly voluntary basis sound instruction "about" religion in the upper levels of secondary school education. Numerous experiments are underway today, with the collaboration of both "liberal" and "conservative" religious groups, to develop sound courses of study about religion, courses to be taught by persons who are well qualified and appropriately certified to do the instruction. In this way, the powerful reality of religious belief and practice would receive more clear-cut recognition in our educational programs, and young persons would gain information, insight, and sensitivity in evaluating their own religious beliefs or their own secular positions.

The problems in arranging for such religious instruction are enormous, of course. The citizenry has a right to be anxious about whether the new group of instructors in religion will in fact be objective and fair in their presentations about religion. It is very easy to slip from instruction to indoctrination, especially in the field of religion, where belief is not a casual thing for any genuinely religious person. As a result, many would insist that it is better not to introduce the teaching about religion even in the higher levels of secondary education, since one simply cannot safeguard the openness and competency of such religious instruction.

The so-called Religious Right, however, is not content with any such academic approaches. For many persons within this Christian coalition, the entire society of the United States must be reclaimed for Christianity (as if it were ever a Christian state!), and the laws of the land must be modified to make that development possible. For some, this means equal treatment of what is called "creation science" alongside of scientific presentations of evolutionary theory. The courts have been consistent in striking down all efforts to require the equal treatment of "creation science," recognizing that the term is a misnomer. The very notion of creation, in the absolute sense of the term, is clearly not a scientific notion. Scientists rightly speculate on the "origin" of the universe, by which they mean how the universe as we know it developed. When the question finally turns, however, to why there is anything rather than nothing, theories may be advanced by any individual or group, but the theories are not in the realm of science. Here is where religious belief enters the picture.

The Religious Right flourishes today largely because of the enormously rapid changes in all features of human life that have occurred during the last fifty years or so. It is very difficult for the human and the moral sensibility to contend with such rapid change. We learn from the effectiveness of the media worldwide what tragedies and monstrous misdeeds are occurring around the globe—and we learn almost instantaneously. Changes in human behavior, in the use of leisure time, in sexual attitudes and practices, in family life, in work habits, and in the understanding and practice of religion have caused great uncertainty and anxiety throughout the entire world. The Religious Right seeks to hold the line, in the midst of such anxious times, for what are taken to be the eternal Christian verities—verities held to be under assault by religious liberals and by much of secular society.

One very valuable outcome of the campaigns of the Religious Right has been its organization to press for public, political consideration of its agenda. Religious liberals have long sought to influence public opinion for what they have taken to be the good of society as a whole, although they maintain that they have not intended to present a set of religious beliefs to be accepted along with their social programs. The Religious Right goes too far when it—apparently—intends to do just that: to present with its social programs a set of religious beliefs and practices that it presses onto the body politic along with its social programs.

As Rabbi Falk has pointed out, Jews and Christians sometimes do not agree on just how religious practitioners should seek to influence the body politic. But both Jews and Christians recognize how important the First Amendment to the United States Constitution is for the health of religion in our society. The state must not favor one religion over another, and the state must not interfere in the practice of religion or in the expression of religious belief, so long as one's religious practice or expression does not interfere with the religious practice or expression of one's neighbor. We have long since learned, however, that matters can get very complicated indeed in the upholding of both of these constitutional provisions.

Jews and Christians need frequently to be reminded that, in religious terms, religious liberty is not just a guarantee of a democratic state; it is the corollary of unswerving belief in the God of Jewish and Christian faith, requiring that we obey God, finally, and not the demands of the state, of our fellow citizens, or even of our ourselves. Bound in covenant to God, we have the gift of religious liberty, and we as citizens need diligently to affirm and protect religious liberty in our secular state.

SUGGESTED READING

Bainton, Roland H. *The Travail of Religious Liberty: Nine Biographical Studies.* Rev. ed. Hamden, Conn.: Archon Books, 1971.
Braybrooke, Marcus. *Stepping Stones to a Global Ethic.* London: SCM, 1992.
Brown, Robert McAfee. *Saying Yes and Saying No: On Rendering to God and Caesar.* Philadelphia: Westminster, 1986.
Faith and Freedom: A Tribute to Franklin H. Littell. New York: Oxford University Press, 1987.
Koshy, Ninan. *Religious Freedom in a Changing World.* Geneva: WCC Publications, 1992.
Kung, Hans. *Global Responsibility: In Search of a New World Ethic.* New York: Crossroads Publishing Co., 1991.
Nicholls, David. *Deity and Domination.* London: Routledge, 1989.
Readings in Church and State. Waco, Tex.; J. M. Dawson Institute of Church-State Studies, 1989.

CHAPTER THREE

RACIAL TENSIONS AND CIVIL RIGHTS

A JEWISH OUTLOOK

Rabbi Leo Baeck, one of the courageous voices of protest against the cruel racism of Hitler's Fascism, expressed the foundation for his belief in the equality of all human beings, when he wrote in *The Essence of Judaism*: "Above all demarcations of races and nations, castes and classes, oppressors and servants, givers and recipients, above all delineations even of gifts and talents stands one certainty: Man. Whoever bears this image is created and called to be a revelation of human dignity."[1] Thus we see, in the very act of creation, that the first ethical principle enunciated in Torah is the equality of all the children of God.

In the Talmud (*Mishnah Sanhedrin* 4:5), the question arises: "Why did God create only one person, Adam?" The answer: "All people are descended from a single human being, Adam, so that no one can say, 'My ancestor is superior to yours.' " Even more on target in the matter of race relations is another talmudic statement (*Yalkut Shimoni* 1:13): "God formed Adam from the dust of all the corners of the earth—yellow (clay) and white (sand), black (loam) and red (soil)." Therefore, no race of humankind can maintain that it preceded or was favored over another, for all were created at the same moment in the first man whom God created.

One of the major themes that echoes throughout the Torah is the lesson learned by the Hebrew tribes' experiences as strangers and as a minority in strange lands. "When an alien resides with you in your land, you shall not oppress the alien. The alien who resides with you

1. Leo Baeck, *The Essence of Judaism*, rev. ed. (New York: Schocken Books, 1987) 152.

shall be to you as the citizen among you; you shall love the alien as yourself, for you were aliens in the land of Egypt: I am the LORD your God" (Lev. 19:33-34). And again in Leviticus: "You shall have one law for the alien and for the citizen: for I am the LORD your God" (Lev. 24:22). "Stranger," of course, refers to any alien, and could be a person of a different race or nation. All strangers are often referred to as "sons of Noah," because it was with Noah that God established the first universal covenant based on the seven Noahite laws.

The Jews' concern for the stranger, who is a minority person within the Jewish community, comes primarily from the historical experience of having been a minority in the land of Egypt, where the Hebrews were enslaved and treated cruelly, because the ruling authorities feared that the minority might grow in numbers and power and challenge the authority of the majority.

Concern for persons of other races, nations, or religions in Jewish tradition is also grounded in our belief in one universal God. This is illustrated so magnificently in the book of Jonah in Hebrew Scriptures. When Jonah is called by God to go to the people of Nineveh to warn them of their forthcoming destruction by God unless they change their evil ways, Jonah is reluctant to be an instrument for saving a people he regards as an enemy. God's concern for all peoples and God's determination that Jonah will be the instrument for salvation of the Ninevites will not be thwarted, however. So Jonah ultimately finds himself at Nineveh to bring God's warning and to save this people. Jews read this lesson on Yom Kippur, the holiest day in our religious calendar, to challenge the Jewish congregations to accept the mission of bringing God's word of salvation for all peoples, even to one's enemies. And, of course, this emphasis on the brotherhood and sisterhood of all humankind reaches its climax in the words of the prophet Malachi: "Have we not all one father? Has not one God created us? Why then are we faithless to one another, profaning the covenant of our ancestors?" (2:10).

This concern for the rights and the welfare of racial, national, and religious minorities has been and continues to be basic to the relationships of Jews and other peoples, both in the state of Israel and in the Diaspora. In the Jerusalem Talmud, a *halacha* ("law") is set forth, establishing a standard by which Jewish communities should treat minorities. This standard is called "for the sake of peace." One practical application of this standard is that when Jews and non-Jews live together in a community, they should collect charity and administer it together, so that they assist Jews and non-Jews alike for the sake of peace in their community (J. Talmud, *Demai* 24a). This law teaches that without sharing the social and economic benefits suggested in the Talmud, the people would generate bitterness that would undermine the positive communal relations indispensible to Jewish values.

In their excellent book *Tough Choices*, Vorspan and Saperstein point out that to this day:

> a priority concern of synagogue social action and of Jewish community relations has been the protection and enhancement of equal rights and equal opportunities for all persons, and the creation of conditions that contribute to vital Jewish living. The security of the Jewish group, as of all groups, rests on the foundation of full equality, individual rights, and personal liberties for all, without regard to race or religion.
>
> Jews have been in the forefront of the struggle to achieve equality of opportunity for African Americans, Hispanics, Asians, and members of all groups suffering from discrimination. Jews recognize that discrimination against any racial or religious group in American life threatens the ultimate security of the Jew. More important for our purposes is the view that Judaism, to fulfill itself, must exert the full weight of its moral prestige toward the achievement of equal rights and opportunities for all persons regardless of race or national origin. For this principle is the essence of our religious faith, as it is the essence of democracy itself.[2]

For many years the African American-Jewish alliance stood firm, and we were united in our efforts to protect the rights of minorities and to enlarge the scope of the civil rights movement. Jews were in the forefront of those who supported financially and through personal participation the National Association for the Advancement of Colored People, the Southern Christian Leadership Conference, the Student Non-Violent Coordinating Committee, and the Leadership Conference on Civil Rights. Symbolic of the close relationship

2. Albert Vorspan and David Saperstein, *Tough Choices: Jewish Perspectives on Social Justice* (New York: UAHC Press, 1992), 9.

of African Americans and Jews in this common struggle was a man like Kivie Kaplan, a charter member of the NAACP and one of its early presidents, and at the same time a vice-chair of the Union of American Hebrew Congregations, especially active in its Social Action Commission. It was in the Kivie Kaplan Religious Action Center in Washington, D.C., that the Civil Rights Act of 1964 and the Voting Rights Act of 1965 were drafted. When Kaplan died, he left a substantial sum of money to the NAACP and the UAHC to establish a joint Institute on Black-Jewish relationships. Unfortunately, despite valiant efforts by some leaders in both organizations, the work of the Institute never got off the ground.

There were also some basic issues on which Blacks and Jews were sharply divided, both within their own organizations and in relationships between the two minorities. One of the most crucial issues was affirmative action. The vast majority of Blacks feel that affirmative action is the only path that will lead ultimately to equal economic opportunity for them. Most Jews feel that affirmative action will lead to the return of the quota system in business and in education, and having fought so long to eliminate quotas, they are reluctant to endorse a policy that would appear to legitimate quotas. Certainly Jewish tradition would oppose any program that gave special favor to one group or another, based on the verse in the book of Leviticus, in which we read: "You shall not render an unjust judgment; you shall not be partial to the poor or defer to the great: with justice you shall judge your neighbor" (Lev. 19:15). Although most Jewish civic defense organizations feel that affirmative action is not the solution to the Blacks' economic and educational problems, the Social Action Commission of the UAHC and the National Council of Jewish Women passed resolutions supporting affirmative action. This did not satisfy the Black leadership, however, for they are convinced that most Jews are not concerned with improving the situation of Black persons in the workplace and on college campuses.

One of the problems that came with affirmative action was that of reverse discrimination. The classic example of this is the DeFunis case, which, like similar landmark cases, eventually reached the Supreme Court. DeFunis, a Jewish student who had applied for admission to the Washington University Law School, felt that he was a victim of reverse discrimination because the university, in an effort to bring more women and racial minorities into its student body, had accepted a Black student whose qualifications were not equal to those of DeFunis. Though the U.A.H.C. Commission on Social Action supported the university in its affirmative action program, the general reluctance of most Jewish organizations to support this stand was responsible, in part, for the breakup of the old Black-Jewish civil rights coalition. However, on other issues many Blacks and Jews have been part of a civil rights coalition in the late 1980s and in the 1990s that has succeeded in expanding civil rights coverage with the extension of the Voting Rights Act, the Fair Housing Act, the Japanese Reparations Act, the Americans with Disabilities Act, and the Civil Rights Act of 1991.

Another area of tension between Blacks and Jews is in the integration of public schools. Though virtually all Jewish national organizations and Jewish rabbinic and lay leaders support the integration of public schools, the fact remains that Jews are a part of the white flight from the public schools with the introduction of busing and other regulations that support integration.

The UAHC attempted to solve this dilemma by passing a resolution at its biennial convention in 1985, holding that "its commitment to public schools should not preclude its support for legitimate efforts to strengthen Jewish education through the option of day schools. Such support, however, was predicated on two conditions: first, that synagogues undertake efforts to strengthen the public schools in their communities, and second, that the movement reaffirm its commitment to separation of church and state, including opposition to federal aid to full-time religious education."[3]

In more recent times, both the Black and the Jewish communities have been divided within their respective groups over the matter of busing. Some Black persons feel that Black children, especially in the elementary grades, have borne the brunt of busing and have suffered from being removed from their neighborhood environment. Many white parents also feel that busing has been disruptive in the loss of school time and school financing for educational purposes. Unquestionably, the opposition to busing has clouded the school integration issue. Recognizing that preparation for economic security depends

3. Ibid., 22.

on a sound, integrated school system, Jews and Blacks alike are exploring ways in which to achieve our common goals, with busing occupying a much less important role in the process. Further development of magnet schools and comprehensive middle and high schools may provide at least a more significant answer, as more of these schools are developed. It is also to be hoped that the Fair Housing Act will contribute greatly to more integrated neighborhoods, which would allow for neighborhood schools that will be naturally integrated rather than artificially integrated through busing.

Still another major area of tension in race relations is the Black anti-Semitism that has been generated by the issues previously discussed. It also has been fueled by the participation of many Blacks in Third World opposition to the state of Israel, and by the Blacks' perception of close economic partnership between Israel and the former political regime in South Africa.

Sympathy from Blacks for the plight of Palestinians is certainly understandable. What is difficult to understand, however, is that responsibility for the plight of the stateless Palestinians is focused almost entirely on the state of Israel. This perspective ignores the fact that Palestinians are refugees from Jordan (despite the majority of Jordanians being Palestinian Arabs), from Syria, from Egypt, from Lebanon, and from Kuwait. While Palestinians and Israelis are slowly moving toward establishment of a Palestinian state, it must be understood that no final solution of the Palestinian problem can be effected without the cooperation and participation of the surrounding Arab states. Until Arab nations, especially Syria, work toward elimination of Arab terrorism, and until the Palestinian issues are recognized as an Arab, as well as an Israeli, concern, there can be no peace in the Middle East. It is important for African Americans to understand both sides of this difficult international problem.

By the same token, it is essential that African Americans recognize that although Israel did, indeed, trade with the apartheid government of South Africa, Israel's percentage of the South African market was infinitesimal compared to that undertaken by the Arab nations, as well as by many European countries. African Americans are too often the victims of propagandists who seek to pit minority against minority for their own ulterior purposes. This, then, brings us to the question of who the leaders are in increasing racial tensions in the Black-Jewish relationship in the United States.

In 1992, the Anti-Defamation League published an important research report: "The Anti-Semitism of Black Demagogues and Extremists." It carefully documented the anti-Semitic statements of Louis Farrakhan, the Rev. Al Sharpton, Prof. Leonard Jeffries, and many others. It focused especially on the anti-Semitism engendered by many Black faculty members and students on college campuses. Black bigots have followed the old anti-Semitic patterns of using the fraudulent "Protocols of the Elders of Zion" and the "International Jew" to incite fear and hatred among Black students. It should also be noted that many Black teachers, clergypersons, and political leaders have repudiated the anti-Semitism being engendered by these persons and by those who are using the old fascist techniques developed by Adolf Hitler in Germany. Important Black leaders like Dr. Martin Luther King, Jr., Barbara Jordan, Professor Henry Louis Gates, Jr., Professor Julius Lester, and many others have repudiated anti-Semitism, and they have done much to counteract the impact of Black anti-Semites. The Congressional Black Caucus has also consistently allied itself with the state of Israel and with the concerns of American Jewry.

Efforts to reduce racial tensions between Blacks and Jews have been effective in many communities throughout the country. In 1991, the Religious Action Center of Reform Judaism, through its Marjorie Kovler Institute for Black-Jewish relations, published a manual on cooperative programming in Black churches and Jewish synagogues. Of the 250 programs described in the report, the following provide some insight into the kind of cooperative activities that were most successful:

> In Los Angeles, Black and Jewish doctors, nurses, and congregants sponsor an annual health fair that serves over three hundred people with basic checkups, blood work, referrals to city agencies, and follow-ups with local clinics.
> In Hamden, Connecticut, a Black church and a Jewish synagogue have founded an interfaith AIDS network that provides financial and emotional support for people living with AIDS.
> In Plainfield, New Jersey, a Black Episcopal church and a Reform

synagogue jointly bought a dilapidated building and, with their own hands, rehabilitated it to house low-income families.

In Manhasset and Great Neck, Long Island, the Black and Jewish communities created summer employment workshops to teach teens job-hunting skills. The same coalition also closed down a crack house that threatened the safety of a local housing project.[4]

Projects such as these certainly are important contributions to the communities in which they are developed. Equally important is the fact that they are effective in cementing Black-Jewish relations. It is also necessary for the Black churches to help their members see the relationship between liberation theology and the Hebrews' struggle from slavery to freedom as told in the book of Exodus. Black clergy need also to dispel the image of Jews as Christ killers, which provides a religious basis for Black anti-Semitism.

By the same token, Jews must seek to eliminate the stereotypes that continue to foster the image of Blacks as lacking a cultural heritage and an educational focus equal to that of Jews. Recent attempts to ascribe a genetic basis for Black inferiority in educational aptitudes must be repudiated by all who recognize the prejudicial basis for such charges.

In seeking to reduce tensions between Blacks and Jews, it is essential that contacts be developed between Jews and Muslims, including the Black Muslim movement. Muslims and Jews also have a common ground in our religious histories and teachings. Interfaith dialogues and community undertakings for Jews and Muslims can do much to provide a foundation for respect of our shared heritage and our spiritual goals.

The influx of Hispanics and Asians into the United States in the last decades of the twentieth century poses new challenges in race relations. Unfortunately tensions between Blacks and newly arrived Hispanics and Asians have increased greatly because of economic competition, primarily in low-income areas. Jews have been affected by these economic conflicts to a lesser degree, but Jews must remember that without a common history, common language, or common religious roots, we have no natural basis for relationship with Asians and Hispanics. Because these minorities will also become important

4. Ibid., 31.

factors in the political and social structures of society, it behooves Jews to reach out a helping hand to these new arrivals and to develop areas in which these minorities can share with Jews our emphasis on strong family life and on efforts to maintain cultural traditions in this pluralistic society.

In seeking to foster better race relations in this country, we cannot overlook an essential outreach to Native Americans. While neither Blacks nor Jews have a basis for shared cultural or religious ties with Native Americans, these largely underprivileged Native American communities deserve our concern and support. We need to learn from history that so long as any minority is deprived of equal opportunity in education or economic security, no minority can take for granted the freedom it cherishes. The very essence of democracy is protection of minority rights. Those minorities that have benefited from this focus in American life must provide leadership and support for all other minorities still seeking to enjoy equal opportunity in the United States of America. As Martin Luther King, Jr., pointed out, whatever affects one minority, affects them all indirectly.

Unfortunately, many minority leaders and spokespersons tend to focus only on the wrongs committed against their own race, nation, or religion. The result is that we become insensitive to the plight of other minorities and fail to stand together when the basic rights of any group are violated. The Hebrew prophets' greatest contribution to humanity was the discovery of the evil of indifference. Amos, First Isaiah, and Micah castigated the people repeatedly for their indifference to the plight of the poor, the orphaned, the widow, and especially the *ger*, the stranger within their gates. By *ger*, the prophets meant persons from other nations who constituted a minority group within the land. Abraham Heschel wrote that "indeed, the major activity of the prophets was *interference*, remonstrating about wrongs inflicted on other people, meddling in affairs which were seemingly neither their concern nor their responsibility. . . . The prophet is a person who is not tolerant of wrongs done to others, who resents other people's injuries. . . . Indifference to evil is more insidious than evil itself; it is more universal, more contagious, more dangerous."[5]

5. Abraham J. Heschel, *The Insecurity of Freedom* (Philadelphia: The Jewish Publication Society of America, 1966), 92.

The prophet Micah, in his magnificent plea for the universal brother-hood of nations under the One God, concluded with the vision that:

> "[God] shall judge between many peoples,
>   and shall arbitrate between strong nations far away;
> . . . .
> nation shall not lift up sword against nation,
>   neither shall they learn war any more;
> but they shall all sit under their
>   own vines and under their own fig trees,
>   and no one shall make them afraid." (Mic. 4:3-4)

In his book *The Moral Core of Judaism and Christianity*, Daniel C. Maguire defines the role of the prophet as one who seeks justice for the disempowered and who shocks a nation into healthy guilt by exposing the outrageousness of prejudice.[6] If African Americans, Jews, and other minorities are to take seriously the challenge of the prophets, then together we must all oppose efforts to curtail the basic civil rights guaranteed in the Constitution and the Bill of Rights.

Joseph C. Hough, Jr., stated this so well in his address on "Responding to Diversity," presented to the men and women of Leadership Nashville. He pointed out that ethnocentrism, which psychologists explain is a natural fear that is exhibited from infancy to adulthood of any thing or person that is strange, is one of the serious obstacles to good group relationships. He also explained that assimilation, which seeks to eliminate differences by absorbing minorities into a majority culture, is not a satisfactory response to differences.

Hough maintains that "engagement is the only strategy that will allow us to celebrate our differences while remaining proud of who we are and from whence we came." Such engagement involves encounter, candid conversation, and mutual respect. Dean Hough reminds us that Martin Buber taught that creative and ethical living requires that we affirm the spirit of the other in such a way that the other one is transformed from an "it" (an object) to a "thou" (a person whose spirit can encounter our spirit). This existential approach to

---

6. Daniel C. Maguire, *The Moral Core of Judaism and Christianity* (Minneapolis: Fortress Press, 1993) 192.

intergroup relationships can provide a foundation for more harmonious racial, ethnic, and religious approaches to civil rights and religious liberty.

One final area of civil rights remains for our consideration. Women's rights and their equality in every aspect of life is of primary importance in Jewish life. In an introduction to a resolution on International Women's Rights, passed at the 1994 convention of the Central Conference of American Rabbis, this statement presents the historic Jewish position on women's rights:

> While Judaism has not historically granted women equal rights under traditional halacha (law), Jewish tradition has recognized from the beginning that women were created equal to men in the most fundamental sense—"in the Divine image . . . male and female God created them and blessed them." (Genesis 1:27). In addition, violence against women was prohibited by our sages; marital rape was forbidden (Talmud, Eruvim 100b), and authorities from Rabbi Meir of Rothenberg (*Responsa Even Ha-ezer* 297, 298, 718-C) to Rabbi Moses Isserles (*Shulkan Aruch*, 153-4) unambiguously condemned esposal abuse, physical or verbal. Furthermore, the traditional Ketubah (marriage contract), while not egalitarian, protected other economic rights of women. Also, though women were traditionally unable to serve as legal witnesses, they were given equal protection under economic contracts and were allowed to inherit when there were not male heirs (Numbers 27:8).

It should be added that in Proverbs 31:10-31, there is a magnificent tribute to the role of women in the home and in the marketplace in biblical times. In the book of Esther, the importance of a woman's courage, when placed in a politically sensitive situation, is highlighted in the first instance of anti-Semitism, manifested in political scapegoatism, in Jewish history. The book of Ruth focuses on the loyalty of a convert to Judaism and the consideration she received as a widow from her adopted family.

One of the six divisions of the Talmud is devoted to the rights of women. Adin Steinsaltz in his book, *The Essential Talmud*, concludes his chapter on the status of women in the Talmud with this statement:

> The talmudic sages did not regard women as inferior creatures but, as one sage succinctly put it, "as a nation apart." They assumed that

there was a separate feminine network of ideas, rules, and guidelines for conduct differing from that of men. And although women were exempted from many of the important precepts that men were obliged to observe, they were not regarded as less important from the purely religious point of view. It was even said that "the Holy One, Blessed be He, made a greater promise for the future of women than to men." The distinction between the sexes is based on functional division of tasks, which are seen as separate but equal.[7]

Of course, Judaism's concern for women's rights has advanced far beyond the concerns in the biblical and talmudic periods. Treatment of women in Jewish life was far better than that found in most other cultures in the ancient and the medieval worlds. Modern history continues to record Jewish involvement in obtaining additional basic human rights for women, based on our tradition of consideration and respect for women and their place in society. Records of the Central Conference of American Rabbis reveal that this rabbinic body was in the forefront of the campaign to obtain the vote for women, to campaign for equal job opportunities for women at equal pay, and to offer women equal educational opportunities, especially in graduate schools focused on the education of physicians, attorneys, engineers, and executives in business management.

It was in 1972 in Cincinnati, Ohio, that the Hebrew Union College-Jewish Institute of Religion ordained the first woman rabbi in almost four thousand years of Jewish history. Each succeeding rabbinic class has seen an increasing number of female rabbinic students, as is true with its cantorial students as well. Now almost half of those admitted to rabbinic and cantorial classes in the Reform movement each year are women. Both the Conservative and the Reconstructionist movements in American Jewish life also ordain women as rabbis and the Conservative movement as cantors too. It is highly improbable that the Orthodox Jews will ever give women equality in religious worship, either as rabbinic or as lay participants.

Women in the American rabbinate today occupy solo pulpits in many congregations and have leadership responsibilities in their respective rabbinical bodies. Lay women also are serving as presi-

7. Adin Steinsaltz, *The Essential Talmud* (New York: Basic Books, 1976) 144.

dents of congregations and in many other significant roles in congregational life. The recently revised prayerbook for Reform congregations uses only gender-neutral terms. *Mankind* becomes *humankind; fathers* becomes *ancestors* or *fathers and mothers;* and references to God have become gender-neutral as well.

Although much is still to be done to ensure complete equality for women in America, the emphasis in the CCAR's resolution adopted at the 1994 convention was on international women's rights:

> Throughout the world, women are discriminated against and suffer intolerable abuses because of their gender. All too often, they are denied such fundamental freedoms as the right to vote, travel freely, testify in court, inherit property, choose a spouse and obtain custody of their children. In addition, women have unequal access to education, employment, health care, and even food. As a result, 70 per cent of the world's rapidly growing poverty-stricken population is female. Furthermore, women worldwide are subject to such abuses as domestic violence, rape, forced prostitution, and other forms of exploitation. . . . This unequal treatment is more than a matter of the denial of abstract rights—it is a matter of life and death. . . . In the words of the United Nations Convention on the Elimination of all forms of Discrimination against Women (CEDAW), such discrimination "violates the principles of equality of rights and respect for human dignity."[8]

The CCAR resolution on International Human Rights concluded by calling upon the United States to ratify the U.N.'s CEDAW and by commending Canada for having done so. It called upon the governments of the United States and Canada to: (1) consider a nation's record on human rights, including women's rights, in determining foreign-aid packages, trade agreements, and other forms of assistance; (2) seek a higher level of United Nations commitment to women's equality as a human right; and (3) ensure that discussion of the human rights of women is included in all relevant global conferences.

In the final analysis, alleviation of racial tensions, expansion of civil rights, and continued pursuit of women's rights all hinge on our recognition of the equality of all human beings under the One God of all humankind. In speaking of justice in basic civil rights—

8. CCAR Yearbook, vol. CIV, pp. 116-18.

including racial, ethnic, religious, and women's rights—Abraham Heschel put it best when he wrote that such "justice is nothing less than God's stake in history. If life is clay, justice is the mold in which God wants history to be shaped."[9]

9. Abraham J. Heschel, *The Prophets* (Philadelphia: The Jewish Publication Society of America, 1962) 198.

SUGGESTED READING

Heschel, Abraham J. *The Insecurity of Freedom*. Philadelphia: The Jewish Publication Society of America, 1966.

Heschel, Abraham J. *The Prophets*. Philadelphia: The Jewish Publication Society of America, 1962.

Maguire, Daniel C. *The Moral Core of Judaism and Christianity*. Minneapolis: Fortress Press, 1993.

Sacks, Maurie, ed. *Active Voices: Women in Jewish Culture*. Chicago: University of Illinois Press, 1995.

Silberman, Charles E. *Crisis in Black and White*. New York: Random House, 1964.

Steinsaltz, Adin. *The Essential Talmud*. New York: Basic Books, 1976.

Vorspan, Albert and David Saperstein. *Tough Choices: Jewish Perspectives on Social Justice*. New York: UAHC Press, 1992.

RACIAL TENSIONS AND CIVIL RIGHTS

A CHRISTIAN OUTLOOK

One of the most shameful features of Christian life worldwide and throughout history has been the justification of racial superiority on the basis of the Bible and the Christian gospel. It may be difficult for persons today to imagine that otherwise honorable and thoughtful Christians, on into the twentieth century, found biblical and theological justification for racial segregation and for the inferiority of peoples of color to those who were white. But as Rabbi Falk has pointed out, just such justification did in fact spread throughout Christian communities.

It should also be pointed out, however, that one of the most splendid chapters in Christian history has been the success realized by African American Christians—of course, with the help of the courts, the federal government, other Christian groups and individuals, and other religious groups—in bringing to an end the "legal" segregation of Blacks and whites in the Southern states. The irony is, however, that the churches, both white and African American, remain almost as segregated as they were before the end of legal segregation. The majority of white congregations continue to have almost no African American members, and most African American congregations are likely to have only a sprinkling of non-Black members. We should note that Roman Catholic and Anglican/Episcopal churches have been somewhat more successful in overcoming segregation, well before the end of "legal" segregation.

It is also the case, as we know, that the gains made by African Americans and other groups whose members are underrepresented in various vocations and professions are, indeed, small, even if they are significant. Our society continues to be marked by prejudices and

74

conventions that effectively keep African Americans and other minorities from an equal sharing in the benefits of citizenship. Women have made greater gains and are holding on to those gains, but women too are far from sharing equally in the fruits of American society, as are other underrepresented groups—Latin Americans and Asian Americans, for example.

THE BIBLE AND CIVIL RIGHTS

Rabbi Falk has laid out many of the foundation points in the Bible and in Jewish tradition that have contributed markedly to the search for equality and justice for all peoples. Those points apply also for the Christian community, of course, although there are some shades of difference. And for both Judaism and Christianity, the term *civil rights*, important and appropriate as it is in a presentation of social ethics, puts things in the wrong order. In the Hebrew Scriptures and in the New Testament, it is the love and grace of God, who found Israel "like grapes in the wilderness" (Hos. 9:10), that is the foundation for Israel's and the church's commitment to civil rights. Both Jews and Christians are committed to those rights conferred upon them and others by the love of God—the right to claim and enjoy the sort of life God purposes for and demands of all those created in the divine image. Once again, we can see that the claim of God upon all human beings is the defining reality. Jews and Christians can and do affirm the secular notion of civil rights—those realities to which human beings are entitled by virtue of their humanity and their membership in a given society, rights spelled out in the Bill of Rights of the United States Constitution and also presented in much greater detail in the International Declaration of Human Rights of the United Nations. But the *religious* grounding of civil rights is of a different order than those. It is perhaps best to specify *what God is entitled to expect of those who live in covenant with God*. God has a "right" to expect of members of the Jewish and Christian communities that they will follow the demands of covenant faith; that they will practice justice as individuals, as members of a religious community, and as citizens of a given state; that they will treat all human beings with the respect they are entitled to as persons created in the image and likeness of God (Gen. 1:26), as those whom God has charged to care for the earth and for one another; and that they will not let prejudice or selfishness or ethnic or family preference get in the way of dealing responsibly with all human beings. Jews and Christians can claim *religiously* that God has a right to expect such conduct from all human beings, for all are created in the divine image and are loved and cared for by God. But for the Jewish and Christian communities, the bond of covenant underscores and defines such "rights" on God's part. For Jews and Christians, God's "right" to expect these things is unmistakable and inescapable.[1]

Christians have the powerful example of Jesus as reported in the Gospels. Over and over again, Jesus appears as the friend of sinners and outcasts (Mark 1:23-27, 40-45), as one who takes the side of the weak against that of the strong (Mark 9:33-37), as one who cautions against the following of traditions and religious customs that may, in given instances, no longer serve the best ends of individuals or the community, and as one who like the prophets before him warns of the amassing of goods and wealth by unjust means and ignoring the needs of the poor.

Christians also have sets of summary ethical guidelines from the letters of Paul, from the classic moral teachings of Jesus found in the Sermon on the Mount (Matthew 5–8), and from Paul's complex Letter to Philemon, which may indeed call into question the very institution of slavery as it is known in the ancient world. The import of these New Testament guidelines is clear: Human beings are created in God's image and are entitled to be treated as persons of incalculable value to God and are, therefore, demanding of honor and respect from all who know themselves to be in covenant with God. To be a Christian is to be committed to the view that race and class and economic status and cultural standing do not and must not count in one's dealings with another human being.

We must be clear, however, that there are two levels of grounding of such an understanding. The society to which one belongs may be committed to such understandings because it affirms the tenets of Christianity or Judaism or Islam, or (more likely) because it is committed to justice and equality in the treatment of all its citizens. As a member of such a society, I will want to affirm this part of my community's heritage and philosophy. But as a *Christian* member of

1. I have outlined this point in *The Ten Commandments and Human Rights* (Philadelphia: Fortress Press, 1980).

that society, I have other motives for affirming the rights and dignity to which all human beings are committed: Christian faith teaches me that God, who loved the whole world so deeply as to send the Son of God for the world's redemption, has laid a special claim upon my life to display that love of God in all my dealings with all human beings. I may find it entirely appropriate to deal with my Christian community in special ways, as my extended family (see chapter 1), but the love with which God loved me and my community is to be extended also and equally to the entire human race—indeed, to the whole of God's creation, human and nonhuman.

RACIAL TENSIONS WITHIN THE CHRISTIAN COMMUNITY

History teaches us, however, that early in the Christian community this divine summons to love all God's people and this demand to extend and display God's love for all in the daily life of Christian individuals and communities were very hard to realize. Even within the inner circle of the disciples of Jesus there were conflicts and desires for preferential treatment (see Mark 9:33-37 and parallels in Matthew and Luke). During Jesus' trial and execution, disciples who had been closest to him denied that they had ever known him (see Mark 15:66-72).[2]

In Paul's letters and in the sketch of the different churches of Asia Minor given in the book of Revelation we learn that conflicts within the Christian congregations were everywhere in evidence. Even in the earliest community following the Resurrection, as portrayed in the early chapters of the book of Acts, not much time elapses before members of the community renege on their commitment to turn over all their property to be held in common for the good of all. At the same time, the demands of God as presented by the risen Christ through the Holy Spirit serve within the Christian community to provide a powerful incentive to equal treatment of all human beings because God's love is extended equally to all human beings.

In this connection we meet once again the dynamism of the Christian ethic. Christians have been able to convince themselves,

2. No such denial on the part of the women who followed Jesus is reported in the Gospels.

for a time, and repeatedly throughout history, that certain forms of human behavior were acceptable—behavior that we now recognize to be clearly in conflict with God's love for all human beings. But they cannot forever escape God's demand that the Christian treat with equal respect and with justice both those who are members of one's kinship group, one's race, one's congregation, one's nation and also those who belong to another family or race or congregation or nation.

THE CENTRALITY OF BIBLICAL TEACHING

Some recent theological thought, however, has tended to play down the value or importance of biblical teaching on contemporary moral questions. For some, the biblical outlook is discredited by its "patriarchy"—that is, its teaching that women are not equal in God's sight with men and that, indeed, much biblical evidence suggests that women were enjoined to accept their role as helpers of men, since they were purposed by God to be subservient to males. On this view, the Bible is a rich and important part of our heritage, but it is not of any real authority in the matters we are discussing in this chapter.

One can sympathize with the anger felt by persons who are drawn to biblical faith, who find it enriching for their lives, but also are repelled by this patriarchy and—even worse—by the failure of biblical texts explicitly to condemn the institution of human slavery. I recall a conversation with a Ph.D. student in Hebrew Bible who was enrolled in a fine seminar on ancient Near Eastern and biblical ethics. The seminar leader had pointed out the remarkable changes made by early Israel in this body of moral teaching as the community of Israel took over many laws and customs from ancient Near Eastern neighbors. The seminar leader showed, for example, how Israel humanized that ethic, focused it on the life and needs of the person and not only the state, and gave much greater protection to the individual than did any of the other societies. The student, nonetheless, was enraged that the seminar leader did not see what a monstrous thing it was that Israel, living in covenant with God, freed from slavery by God's action, had not been able to denounce outright the institution of human slavery. How could we be at ease with such a fact? What difference did it make that ancient Israel *made some improvements* in ancient Near Eastern ethics? Israel did not denounce slavery as an abomination, though it denounced other human acts as abominations in the sight of God! Did they not think that God was appalled at the very existence of human slavery? And if they did not, why not?

That conversation could be multiplied in relation to the Bible's teaching on women, on homosexuality, on ecology. But many feminists and African American biblical interpreters and other students of biblical ethics, while recognizing these limits in the biblical perspective, also find the seeds of human liberation to have developed over the whole course of Jewish and Christian history. The Bible *does* offer a picture of human life as God intends it, a picture in which there is no place for racial conflict or discrimination, where even the covenant people Israel exist to bear God's witness of love and justice to "all the families of earth" (Gen. 12:3). God does not discriminate or play favorites, although God's love is displayed in a unique way in the covenant between Israel and the deity and between God and the Christian community. An intimacy of relationship, however, does not mean favoritism, and it certainly does not suggest a lack of concern on God's part for all peoples, for the whole of the creation, the universe as such.

RACIAL INJUSTICE OVER THE CENTURIES

Clearly, the Christian community over the centuries has had to struggle with this demand for equality on the part of all persons. The massive experience of the church in dealing with questions of economic justice shows well what the problems are. Once the Christian community became the "official" religion of the Roman Empire toward the end of the fourth century C.E., it was inevitable, humanly speaking, that Christian leaders would accommodate their message to allow for their own privileged status within the empire. Similarly, in the treatment of the European peoples and tribes who were conquered by the empire and those who later proved to be the conquerors, there was much discrimination on the basis of race and class. In given lands, the upper stratum of Christian society saw to it that advancement in the church went to those who belonged to the "right" race or class. It is true that there were persons from the lower strata of society who, on the basis of their sheer ability, came to the highest of offices within the church and within Christian society.

The problem for the church was only compounded by the establishment of so-called Christian states, areas in which the religion of the ruling family or party placed its religion over the entire land. In the breakup of the feudal system during Reformation and Counter-Reformation times, much of value ensued from the doctrine that "the one who rules determines the religion of those ruled" (Latin: *cuius regio, ejus religio*). Some princes of "Christian" states yielded to the authority of religious reformers and established laws that were more just, sought to make peace with their neighbors, supported scholarship and the arts, and became powerful instruments of Christian education and culture. Other princes of Christian states (and all such princes at various times, it seems) simply used religion to justify and enforce state policy, often resorting to fanaticism and unspeakable cruelties in the name of Christian faith.

The Enlightenment and later developments, as we noted above, brought changes for the better to European and other Christian states, enabling them either to provide benign ways to affirm the Christian character of the state (as in Great Britain, Holland, Germany, the Scandinavian lands) or to declare a strict separation of church and state (as in France and the United States).

The modern missionary movements of Europe and North America brought great changes in the nineteenth and the early twentieth centuries. While it was the case that, along with the Christian gospel, European, British, and North American missionaries brought to Africa and Asia and other lands a culture, a social outlook, and an economic system that they took to be superior to what they found, thus bringing the European/American way of life along with the gospel, these missionaries *did indeed* bring the gospel of God's love for all persons equally. They brought the message of the Bible, which, with all its limitations, reinforced this message of God's demand for justice in dealings with all and God's love for all persons, irrespective of race or sex or class or economic status. The missionaries also brought literacy, fresh opportunities, and a system of education that would, in time, enable the people of these colonial states to bring colonialism to an end.[3]

3. See the marvelous autobiography of President Nelson Mandela of South Africa for his account of what the conversion of his family to Christianity did for him. See Nelson Mandela, *Long Walk to Freedom* (Boston: Little, Brown, 1994).

CHRISTIANITY AND THE AMERICAN CIVIL RIGHTS MOVEMENT

The modern civil rights movement was born in the African American church and achieved its most notable successes through the leadership of African American clergy and laypersons. State-mandated segregation of whites and Blacks in many Southern states in the United States, plus the de facto segregation of life in most other parts of the land, was challenged by African American students who simply refused any longer to accept such unjust laws as binding upon them. Like the early Christians of the book of Acts, they too insisted, "We must obey God, not human beings." They sat at lunch counters and demanded service. When service continued to be denied, they sat or they picketed, and they gathered by the thousands in the streets of Southern cities, accompanied by many white supporters. Eventually all state and municipal segregation laws were made inoperative by the 1964 Civil Rights Act, signed into law by President Lyndon B. Johnson. Martin Luther King, Jr., the national leader of this movement, was awarded the Nobel Peace Prize for his witness. Over time, Dr. King's name was to be commemorated in many ways throughout the land, including finally the designation of his birthday as a national holiday.

This twentieth-century prophetic movement built its case upon the Bible—the Jewish and the Christian Bible. Just as God heard the outcry of oppressed slaves in Egypt and came to deliver them, so also God was demanding the end of inequalities based upon race. Just as the nineteenth-century practice of slavery had finally been abolished on the basis of biblical teaching, so also racially segregated life, supported by the laws of the states, was abolished.

Sadly, the desegregation of the school system, the commercial establishments, the universities and colleges, and governmental agencies has not significantly changed living patterns in many parts of the country. The result is that African Americans and whites continue to enjoy very little social and cultural interchange. Saddest of all, the Christian congregations, most of them, have done little to overcome this lack of genuine social and cultural and religious interchange. African American churches learned how important their congregations were to the very life and health of the larger community, and their leaders, understandably, insist on keeping them distinct and strong. And white congregations, often with much relief, have been content to welcome African American members when they come for worship or formally become members, but they have done little to encourage the development of biracial congregations. Only the more liturgical churches have been a bit more successful in overcoming almost total segregation, and those churches too have congregations that are largely white or largely Black.

The racial conflicts of an earlier epoch today tend to be treated not as the unique thing they are but as instances of the continuing mistreatment of minorities within the society. Latin American, Asian American, Native American, and African American communities have had to organize to demand better treatment by American society and within the Christian community. So also have women, gays and lesbians, and persons with handicapping conditions. The hue and cry today over affirmative action, dealt with above by Rabbi Falk, arises largely from the fact that there are so many groups within the society that have been dealt with unfairly by the majority white population that any effort to respond positively to all seems doomed from the outset. White males are said to be indignant over the mistreatment they suffer at the hands of employers, in business, in professional life, in labor unions, in the universities, in government, and in the church as well.

Injustices have surely occurred. The question of just how much ought to be done by the dominant population, those who enjoy the bulk of what a society has to offer, to share the society's opportunities and goods more equitably is, of course, enormously complex. Think only of what it would mean to set out to share the economic goods of the earth fairly among all earth's citizens! Or to devise a fair plan for the use of earth's goods by both the current generation and the generations to come! The continuing value of affirmative action, in my judgment, is its flat acknowledgment that, while we cannot redress all the mistakes and sins of earlier generations, we can do *something* to help lagging minorities catch up. Some of the minorities are, in fact, catching up. Women, if for the purpose of this discussion they can be considered a minority, clearly continue to lag in many areas and are discriminated against in grievous ways by the church (notably by those bodies that will not ordain women to ministry or priesthood). But in other ways women are taking the lead within the society. In most Protestant theological schools, for example, women outnumber men within the student body. They are also gaining in numerical strength on the faculties of the same theological schools. And in Roman Catholic and Anglican theological schools, the numbers of women faculty members and students also grow rapidly, even though priestly ordination continues to be denied Roman Catholic women.

Gays and lesbians, too, are slowly gaining ground in their treatment within the Christian community. Native American, Latin American, and Asian American congregations, still tend to be distinct bodies within the Christian community, with the more liturgical churches finding it easier to develop really inclusive congregations. But among all these "minority" groups, African Americans stand out as being separated more regularly from congregations that are largely white. Can anything be done about this situation? Should it continue to alarm us?

NEW POSSIBILITIES TO EASE RACIAL CONFLICTS

One urgent need within the Christian community today is for congregations that are largely white to commit themselves to identify, if they possibly can, African American families within their community who might find the white congregation appropriate for them to join. The best way to avoid conflict is for an African American and a white congregation to team up and see if the process cannot be made to go both ways—with some white families committing to join the African American congregation and some African American families joining the white congregation. If this act were accompanied by regular exchanges of pulpits between the two congregations, regular congregational meetings to share meals and special mission tasks, then the bonds uniting the families to their original congregation would remain intact even as the families found a new life in the other congregation.

Among the more liturgically oriented congregations, this idea ought to prove equally valuable, for those congregations, even with a larger percentage of minority members, still need to make explicit commitments to the overcoming of the racial divisions that continue to plague our society.

Such steps are made the more urgent by the developments on the national political scene. The attacks on affirmative action, the dismantling of many programs that are especially valuable to African American individuals and families, and the very spirit of hostility toward African Americans that is unmistakable in the land today all show how urgent it is for the Christian community to take steps, in as many ways as possible, to demonstrate that the Christian gospel demands the end of mistreatment of individuals or groups on the basis of race. The Christian community can, of course, continue its life without taking radical steps to help to overcome the continuing segregation of the lives of Black and white Americans. But surely it does not wish to do so.

Those steps that have helped so much to overcome the Christian misunderstanding of Judaism and the mistreatment of Jews have their analogue in the relations of Black and white Christians. Chief among them has been the insistence that we get to know one another, that we work together, that we share life and struggles and study, and in those ways discover just how much we need one another. All of the conflicts within the society where groups are suffering injustice must be addressed. But is any one of them as urgent as the continuing, unfinished task of demanding a Christian community in which African American and white Christians live and work and study and witness together as one people of God?

SUGGESTED READING

Lincoln, C. Eric. *The Black Church in the African-American Experience*. Durham, N.C.: Duke University Press, 1990.

Lewis, W. Arthur. *Racial Conflict and Economic Development*. Cambridge, Mass.: Harvard University Press, 1985.

Locke, Alain LeRoy. *Race Contacts and Interracial Relations: Lectures on the Theory and Practice of Race*. Washington, D.C.: Howard University Press, 1992.

Paris, Peter J. *The Spirituality of African Peoples: The Search for a Common Moral Discourse*.

Shaw, John W. *Strategies for Improving Race Relations: The Anglo-American Experience*. Manchester: Manchester University Press, 1987.

Sinderman, Paul M. *The Scar of Race*. Cambridge, Mass.: Harvard University Press, 1993.

Sowell, Thomas. *Race and Culture: A World View*. New York: Basic Books, 1994.

CHAPTER FOUR

WAR AND PEACE

A JEWISH OUTLOOK

In the past thirty years there have been at least sixty-five major wars on every continent on earth. Almost one-third of the national budget of the United States is allocated for the production of weapons for war and for funding military forces and related agencies to develop methods and strategies to kill more people more efficiently. Indeed, judged by the tremendous sums of money we channel into wars and preparation for wars, and judged by the number of television programs and motion pictures that glorify violence, killing seems to be a basic ingredient in our way of life. It could be the defining characteristic of twentieth-century civilization. No wonder that many prominent clergypersons and psychologists today affirm the statement in the book of Genesis (9:2): "the devisings of man's mind are evil from his youth."[1]

In contrast to this focus on war and violence, Jewish tradition has neither glorified war nor exalted war makers. In Jewish history, the heroes are scholars and sages, rarely warriors. Rabbi Yochanan ben Zakkai is revered for his nonviolent triumph over the mighty Roman Empire, by establishing his academy at Yavneh to assure the continuity of Jewish learning after the fall of Jerusalem. Josephus reminds us also of Jewish nonviolent resistance to the warmonger Caligula. We also learn in Hebrew Scriptures that King David was not permitted by God to build the Temple in Jerusalem because he had been involved as an aggressor in wars to expand the borders of the nation. And every Passover we read in the Haggadah that when the angels in heaven rejoiced that Pharaoh's hosts drowned in the Sea of Reeds,

---

1. See also Bradley S. Artson, *Love Peace and Pursue Peace: A Jewish Response to War and Nuclear Annihilation* (New York: United Synagogue of America, 1988) 15.

God admonished them: "My creatures are perishing and you want to sing praises!" (Talmud, *Megillah* 10b).

Most significantly, the holiday of Hanukkah, based on the account of the Maccabean victory over the Syrian army, as recounted in 1 and 2 Maccabees in the Apocrypha, was largely ignored until comparatively recent times. Only when the emphasis was changed from celebration of a military victory to rejoicing in the restoration and rededication of the Temple in Jerusalem did this become a holiday of major importance in Jewish life. The focus was placed on the Haftorah assigned for reading at Sabbath services during the eight-day holiday celebration: "Not by might, nor by power, but by my spirit, says the LORD" (Zech. 4:6).

Rabbinic teaching not only decries physical violence in conflicts between individuals and between nations, but it also requires active pursuit of peace. The Torah admonishes: "You shall purge the evil from your midst" (Deut. 21:21). This responsibility is amplified in the Talmud, where we are warned: "Whoever is able to protest against the transgressions of the people of his community, and does not do so, is punished for the transgressions of his community. Whoever is able to protest against the transgressions of the entire world and does not do so, is punished for the transgressions of the entire world" (*Shabbat* 54b). Rabbi Abraham Heschel underscored this obligation to confront injustice when he said: "Indifference to evil is more insidious than evil itself."

Because of this emphasis on the obligation to confront evil and injustice, Jewish tradition recognizes that there are situations in which participation in war is a necessity. In the Talmud, wars were classified in two types, the first being obligatory wars. Three types of wars were considered obligatory: the wars that were waged in biblical times to conquer the seven Canaanite nations, thereby securing the land that God had promised, in covenant with the patriarchs and with Moses; the wars to destroy the Amalekites, a tribe that had brutally attacked the Israelites during their forty years in the desert; and wars of national defense when Israel was under attack (Talmud *Sota* 44b).

The second type of war was a "war of permission." Two such kinds of war were considered optional: wars to extend the boundaries of Israel after the land was conquered, and preemptive wars against those who might attack Israel. However, in these optional wars not everyone was required to participate. In Deuteronomy 20:5-9, we find this stipulation:

> Then the officials shall address the troops, saying, "Has anyone built a new house but not dedicated it? He should go back to his house, or he might die in the battle and another dedicate it. Has anyone planted a vineyard but not yet enjoyed its fruit? He should go back to his house, or he might die in the battle and another be first to enjoy its fruit. Has anyone become engaged to a woman but not yet married her? He should go back to his house, or he might die in the battle and another marry her." The officials shall continue to address the troops, saying, "Is anyone afraid or disheartened? He should go back to his house, or he might cause the heart of his comrades to melt like his own." When the officials have finished addressing the troops, then the commanders shall take charge of them.

Jewish tradition not only recognizes two types of war in which Jews may find it necessary to participate, but it also sets forth in Hebrew Scriptures and in the Talmud at least five regulations that serve as limitations to violence and to the destructiveness of war. First, Jews are required never to allow force to become an end in itself. It must only be used as a means of achieving peace. In commenting on this mandate, in the context of nuclear armaments, Rabbi Elliot Holin wrote: "In striving to acquire ultimate power, we are left with a sense of powerlessness. In seeking security, we have discovered greater fear. Indeed, there is no safety in the awesome arsenal we have created, for it rules us and we live in dread under its shadows."[2]

Second, before a battle was launched in biblical times, an opportunity had to be given for the opposing side to choose peace. "When you draw near to a town to fight against it, offer it terms of peace" (Deut. 20:10). The goal of this rule seems to establish a pattern in which warfare may be avoided wherever possible.

Third, in Jewish tradition, there is special concern for the lives of noncombatants. An opportunity for escape must be provided. Therefore, it was decreed that when siege is laid to a city in order to

---

2. See David Saperstein, ed., *Preventing the Nuclear Holocaust: A Jewish Response* (New York: UAHC Press, 1983), 9.

capture it, it may not be surrounded on all four sides, but only on three, to give an opportunity for women, children, and the elderly to escape and flee to save their lives.

Fourth, war could not be waged in such a manner as to destroy the earth and its capability to sustain life. "If you besiege a town for a long time, making war against it in order to take it, you must not destroy its trees. . . . Although you may take food from them, you must not cut them down" (Deut. 20:19-20). The Talmud expands this concept to include a ban on the destruction of other things that are vital to ongoing civilian life; thus there was a prohibition against burning, breaking, or destroying food, clothing, utensils, or other household items (*Talmud Shabbat* 106b).

Finally, before every battle the "Priest Anointed for Battle" had to read to the soldiers the rules and regulations on war (a Jewish equivalent to the Geneva Convention). These regulations provided a clear pattern of conduct in times of war: to destroy human life, to damage this planet, is to act in defiance to God's creation. For this reason, biblical and talmudic law establish these regulations, which seek to minimize such destruction.[3]

These humanitarian rules that attempt to temper the brutality and reduce the suffering that result from war remind us that Jewish teaching emphasizes that the causes of war are most often rooted in deprivation of the basic needs of food, clothing, and shelter that force nations to resort to desperate measures to alleviate the suffering of the masses of people. In this connection, it is interesting to note that the Hebrew word for "war," *milchama*, derives from the word *locham*, which means both "to feed" and "to wage war." The Hebrew word *lechem* ("bread") comes from the same root. The rabbis, therefore, suggest that the lack of bread and other necessities of life is a major factor leading to war. The seeds of war are often found in the inability of a nation to provide adequate food for its people. Thus the sages in *Pirke Avot* (a section of the Mishnah) taught: "The sword comes into the world because of justice delayed, because of justice perverted, and because of those who render wrong decisions" (Mishnah *Pirke Avot* 5:11).

The prophet Hosea suggested that the reason for war was that

---

3. See Saperstein, *Preventing the Nuclear Holocaust*, 6-12.

men glory in their own might and power instead of recognizing that power comes from God:

> Because you have trusted in your power
>   and in the multitude of your warriors,
> therefore the tumult of war shall rise against your people,
>   and all your fortresses shall be destroyed. (Hos. 10:13-14)

The Bible offers a profound observation also on the nature of war: that it tends to replicate itself. For example, Abimelech's subjects, who first rebelled to put him in power, later rebel to remove him. He and the people of Shechem became embroiled in a continuous war. The people in King David's time also provide models of violence in the service of ambition. Perhaps the most prominent of these is David's son Absalom, who rebelled against his father and ultimately lost his life in that same rebellion.

On the other hand, we also learn in Hebrew Scriptures that war sometimes serves a positive political function, in that it can be the price of maintaining and honoring an alliance. In the book of Genesis, we find that Abraham was dragged into a war because his nephew Lot had been taken captive. Although Abraham had no personal interest in the war, his connection to Lot compelled him to fight. Similarly, when Ahab, the king of Israel, wanted to wage war against Aram, a neighboring kingdom, he persuaded the king of Judah to join him, based not on any intrinsic hostility against Aram on the part of Judah, but on the obligations of their alliance (1 Kings 22:1-4).

We cannot overlook the fact that ideology can also be a rational basis for prosecuting a war. A striking example of this is the story in the Apocrypha of the Maccabees and their followers in battle against the Syrians. The amazing victories of the Maccabees were, in some measure, attributable to the intensity of their commitment to the preservation of their Jewish heritage.[4]

To put the various historical approaches to war in perspective from Jewish and Christian traditions, we should examine their respective responses to the Persian Gulf War. Because of general opposition of most Protestant and Catholic leadership in contrast to

4. Artson, *Love Peace and Pursue Peace*, 25-28.

overwhelming approval by Jewish leaders of the participation of the United States in that war, it is important that we understand the similarities and differences between Christian and Jewish "just war" theory. For both Christians and Jews, "just war" involves moral justification for beginning the war, and moral means of fighting the war.

In regard to the moral justification for participation in a war, both Jews and Christians believe that the underlying cause for a war must be just. In both traditions, self-defense or defense of an innocent bystander (in this instance, Kuwait) would be a valid reason. Here, the only difference between the two traditions is the question of who is qualified to declare war. For most Christians, that authority is vested in a president, a king, or a prime minister. Judaism requires a check on the authority of the executive. In ancient times that check came through the Sanhedrin, just as in the United States the approval of Congress is required.

The question of when and how to wage war provides several interesting differences in the Christian and Jewish traditions. Basic Christianity permits use of force only as a last resort. Therefore, most Christian leaders advocated allowing more time for sanctions to work against Iraq prior to a declaration of war. Judaism requires only that a "good faith" effort to avoid war be made. This could mean requiring efforts for a peaceful resolution up to three days before an attack; other *halacha* ("law") requires a country to sue for peace on three consecutive days. The United States seems at least to have met the requirements of Jewish tradition in this regard.

Both Jewish and Christian traditions have a major concern for the protection of civilian life. In the Gulf War, the efforts of the allies to protect women and children were in sharp contrast to the intentional Iraqi attacks on civilian centers of population in Israel and in Kuwait. Christianity requires the test of "proportionality" (how much force is necessary to achieve a given military objective). Judaism is more concerned with which targets are legitimately subject to attack and which are not. Judaism's concern for the protection of the environment by prohibiting the destruction of trees or plants that provide food, as well as storehouses of food, fulfills the requirement of *bal tashcit* ("do not destroy"), found in Deuteronomy 20:19-20. Judaism was concerned that both sides in the Gulf War violated this prohibition, Iraq through dumping millions of barrels of oil into the sea and setting fire to hundreds of oil wells, and the Coalition forces by bombing civilian targets to severely damage the economy, health, housing, and water infrastructure of Iraq.

There is also ample evidence in both the Hebrew Scriptures and in rabbinic teachings in Talmud and Midrash that Jewish military leaders and their sages were truly compassionate in relationships with their enemies. We see this clearly in the words of the prophet Elisha, when he explained to the king of Israel the proper treatment of prisoners of war: "Did you capture with your sword and your bow those whom you want to kill? Set food and water before them so that they may eat and drink; and let them go to their masters. . . . He sent them on their way. . . . And the Arameans no longer came raiding into the land of Israel" (2 Kings 6:22-23).

In the book of Proverbs there are at least two very powerful statements about how enemies should be treated:

> Do not rejoice when your enemies fall,
>   and do not let your heart be glad when they stumble.
> (Prov. 24:17)
> "If your enemies are hungry, give them bread to eat
> And if they are thirsty, give them water to drink."
> (Prov. 25:21)

Unfortunately the Hebrew Scriptures also record many instances in which kings and generals did not follow the admonitions of the sages. However, there is nothing in biblical literature that in any way permits or justifies violation of these concerns for the enemies of Israel.

Rabbinic tradition gives us interesting insights into the way that Joshua dealt with Israel's enemies as they entered the promised land. In *Vayikra Rabbah* (a midrashic commentary on the book of Leviticus in the Hebrew Scriptures), we read:

Joshua had sent to them (the Seven Nation) three proclamations: "Whoever wishes to leave, let him leave; whoever wishes to make peace, let him make peace; whoever wishes to give battle, let him give battle." The Girgashites rose and left of their own accord; as a reward there was given them a land as good as their own land: "I shall come and take you away to a land like your own land" (Isaiah 36:17) namely Africa. The Gibeonites made peace with them, as it is said "the inhabitants of Gibeon had made peace with Israel" (Joshua 10:1). The thirty-one kings made war and were overthrown.

Although Jews have always been concerned for the welfare of their enemies, it would be difficult to categorize Jewish tradition as being pacifistic. We have already cited the Jewish tradition of participation in "just wars." We cannot remain passive before tyranny and injustice. At the same time, nonviolence and peace are ultimate goals of the Jewish people. Isaiah and Micah expressed this best when they wrote:

> they shall beat their swords into plowshares,
> and their spears into pruning hooks;
> nation shall not lift up sword against nation,
> neither shall they learn war any more.

and Micah added:

> but they shall all sit under their
> own vines and under their own fig trees,
> and no one shall make them afraid;
> for the mouth of the LORD of hosts has spoken.
> (Mic. 4:3-4)

This aspiration for peace, however, is not the sole consideration in Jewish thought. Although in the Talmud God is sometimes referred to as *Shalom* ("Peace") God is also called *Ish Milchamah*, the "Lord of War." Just as Isaiah and Micah urge that swords be beaten into plowshares and spears into pruning hooks, the prophet Joel insists that the nation must transform plowshares into swords and pruning hooks into spears. Despite all the prayerful yearnings for peace, neither the prophets nor the sages of the Talmud were pacifists. If war is reprehensible, an unjust peace is immoral.[5]

A pragmatic position consistent with Jewish values today is what Rabbi Albert Axelrod, Hillel Director at Brandeis University, has

---

5. Saperstein, *Preventing the Nuclear Holocaust*, 6.

called the "pacifoid" position. He defines this as one who is "like" or "resembling" or "near" pacifist, that is, a person who joins pacifists in pursuing peace, even while accepting the possibility of fighting if there appears to be no alternative. This would include defending Israel against attack by Arab countries and the Allied resistance to Hitler in World War II.

It must be noted that such a position is not "passivism"—lack of involvement; Jews can act in nonviolent ways in attempting to change unjust conditions.[6]

Can a Jew, then, be classified as a pacifist under any circumstances? The answer is yes, based primarily on the verses from Deuteronomy 20, previously cited. Here we are provided with examples of situations in which men were excused from military service, including when a man is "fearful and fainthearted."

The position of most American Jews vis-à-vis militarism and pacifism is expressed best in a letter sent to the director of the Selective Service System from the Synagogue Council of America (which includes Orthodox, Conservative and Reform congregations) in 1970. The letter stated, in part:

> Jewish faith, while viewing war as a dehumanizing aberration and enjoining a relentless quest for peace, recognizes that war can become a tragic, unavoidable necessity. Judaism is therefore not a pacifist faith in the sense that this term is generally used.
>
> However, this fact does not preclude the possibility of individuals developing conscientious objection to war based on their understanding of and sensitivity to the moral imperatives of the Jewish tradition. In other words, Jewish faith can indeed embrace conscientious objection, and Jewish law makes specific provision for the exemption of such moral objectors.[7]

In 1971, the Synagogue Council expanded on this statement to assert that selective conscientious objection to war is also consistent with Judaism. This was specifically in regard to those men and women who refused to fight in the Vietnam war because they felt that U.S. involvement was illegal and immoral. This additional statement reads:

6. Richard H. Schwartz, *Judaism and Global Survival* (New York: Atara Publishing Co., 1987) 90-91.
7. Ibid., 92.

Judaism considers each individual personally responsible before God for his actions. No man who violates the eternal will of the Creator can escape responsibility by pleading that he acted as an agent of another, whether that other be an individual or the state. It is therefore possible, under unusual circumstances, for an individual to find himself compelled by conscience to reject the demands of a human law which, to the individual in question, appears to conflict with the demand made on him by a higher law.[8]

Above everything except for the gift of life, Judaism stresses the primary obligation to seek peace and to pursue it. The Hebrew word for peace, *shalom*, means much more than a lack of violence. It comes from a root verb that means "wholeness." Thus *shalom* is a state of fulfillment, and the greatest blessing God can bestow is the blessing of peace. Without peace, all other blessings are meaningless. We are also taught in the *Avot DeRabbi Natan*, a midrashic work, that it is not enough to sit silently in your place and enjoy the peace that surrounds you. We must also pursue peace throughout the world, wherever there is strife. We are taught that only when all people can enjoy peace does life become truly complete.

In Hebrew Scripture, God is often portrayed as strongly opposing violence:

"I will break the bow and the sword and the battle out of the land, And will make them to lie down safely."

(Hos. 2:20)

"He maketh wars to cease unto the end of the earth; He breaketh the bow, and cutteth the spear in sunder; He burneth the chariot in the fire." (Ps. 46:9 KJV)

The Rabbis in the Talmud also emphasized that peace was most profoundly to be sought by both the individual and the community. A few examples can indicate the focus on peace in rabbinic thought:

"Great is peace, for God's name is peace, as it is said (Judges 6:25), "And he called the Lord peace.' . . . Great is peace, for it encompasses all blessings. . . . Great is peace, for even in times of war, peace must be sought" (Leviticus Rabbah 9:9).
"Great is peace, seeing that when the Messiah is to come, he will commence with

8. Ibid.

94

peace, as it is said (Isaiah 52:7), "How beautiful upon the mountains are the feet of the messenger of good tidings that announce peace" (Leviticus Rabbah 9:9).

The whole Torah was given for the sake of peace, and it is said (Proverbs 3:17, "all her paths are peace." (Talmud, Gittin 59b)

The issues of war and peace that we face in the last decade of the twentieth century are not very different from those that we have seen the people of Israel confront in biblical times and later in the rabbinic period. What are the crucial challenges that force us to engage in a "just war"? What are the measures we can take to avoid war? Should we seek security through stockpiling cruise missiles and chemical weapons or through feeding the hungry, housing the homeless, securing the health of all people and the education of all children? What is our sense of purpose, based on the ethical standards of our heritage?

Abba Eban, the Israeli statesman, summarized the answer to these questions best when he wrote:

> In each of us and in every nation and every faith, there are arsenals of destructive rage, but there are also powerful armies of moral strength. The choice is ours, even as it has been since these words were addressed to our people: "See, I have set before you this day, the blessing and the curse, life and death; therefore, choose life that you may live, you and your seed after you" (Deuteronomy 30:19).
>
> As we look out on the human condition, our consciences cannot be clean. If they are clean, then it is because we do not use them enough. It is not inevitable that we march in hostile and separate hosts into the common abyss. There is another possibility—of an ordered world, illuminated by reason, governed by law. If we cannot touch it with our hands, let us at least grasp it with our vision.[9]

Finally, we would share a Jewish liturgical foundation for understanding the aspiration for peace in our heritage. Jules Harlow, in his article "Peace in Traditional Jewish Expression," quoted a prayer by Nahman of Bratslav, a late eighteenth- and early nineteenth-century Hasidic Rabbi:

9. Albert Vorspan and David Saperstein, *Tough Choices: Jewish Perspectives on Social Justice* (New York: UAHC Press, 1992) 133.

"May it be Your will, Adonai our God, and God of our ancestors, Master of Peace, Sovereign who possesses peace, to grant peace to your people Israel. And may that peace increase until it extends to all who inhabit the world, so that there is no hatred, jealousy, strife, triumphalism, or reproach between one person and another, so that only love and peace will embrace them all."[10]

SUGGESTED READING

Artson, Bradley S. *Love Peace and Pursue Peace: A Jewish Response to War and Nuclear Annihilation.* New York: United Synagogue of America, 1988.

Good, Robert M. "The Just War in Ancient Israel." *Journal of Biblical Literature* 104, 3 (1985).

Gordon, Haim. "Beyond Fatalism: Education for Peace Within Judaism." In *Education for Peace: Testimonies from World Religions.* Edited by H. Gordon and L. Grob. Marynoll, N.Y.: Orbis, 1987.

Grob, Leonard. "Pursuing Peace: Shalom in the Jewish Tradition." In *Education for Peace: Testimonies from World Religions.* Edited by H. Gordon and L. Grob. Marynoll, N.Y.: Orbis, 1987.

Saperstein, David, ed. *Preventing the Nuclear Holocaust: A Jewish Response.* New York: UAHC Press, 1983.

Schwartz, Richard H. *Judaism and Global Survival.* New York: Atara Publishing Co., 1987.

Vorspan, Albert, and David Saperstein. *Tough Choices: Jewish Perspectives on Social Justice.* New York: UAHC Press, 1992.

10. Artson, *Love Peace and Pursue Peace,* x.

WAR AND PEACE

A CHRISTIAN OUTLOOK

"You have heard that it was said, 'An eye for an eye and a tooth for a tooth.' But I say to you, Do not resist an evildoer. But if anyone strikes you on the right cheek, turn the other also; and if anyone wants to sue you and take your coat, give your cloak as well; and if anyone forces you to go one mile, go also the second mile. Give to everyone who begs from you, and do not refuse anyone who wants to borrow from you.

"You have heard that it was said, 'You shall love your neighbor and hate your enemy.' But I say to you, Love your enemies and pray for those who persecute you, so that you may be children of your Father in heaven; for he makes his sun rise on the evil and on the good, and sends rain on the righteous and on the unrighteous."(Matt. 5:38-45)

"Blessed are the peacemakers, for they will be called children of God." (Matt. 5:9)

These quotations from the Sermon on the Mount set the tone for this effort to interpret the Christian perspective on war and peace. There can be no doubt that Jesus spoke strongly against violence, including efforts to overthrow the Roman occupation of Palestine by force. One recent careful study of the Gospel record concludes that a central feature of Jesus' message to his followers was, from first to last, "Do not attempt to gain your political freedom by resorting to acts of violence. They are not necessary, and they are sure to bring disaster." In place of violence, the author contends, Jesus called on his followers to be imaginative, bold, and unyielding in their resistance to injustice and mistreatment, working for public and private justice, but simply refusing to lift up their hands against the authorities, or against anyone else,

97

violently. Jesus preached the nearness, the coming, the at-handness of the nonviolent kingdom of God.[1]

Other groups through the centuries have reached the same conclusion but without claiming that the Gospels themselves point to such a politically active social program on Jesus' part, marked by nonviolence. The "Peace Churches" through the centuries have generally fixed upon such texts as those quoted above and have been confident that they were following Jesus' teaching and Jesus' way in the world by their own basic commitment to nonviolence and to peacemaking in the name of Christ.

In recent times, other Christian theologians and ethicists have taken a different approach. For them, the Western Christian church has virtually submerged itself in the larger society of Western Europe and North America, leaving itself with little or no distinctive word of life or hope for a society bent upon its own enjoyment, the pursuit of its own interests, even in the face of desperate social and economic need worldwide. These Christian thinkers propose to take up a theme from Paul, who spoke of the church as having its citizenship (or "commonwealth") in heaven (Phil. 3:20). The church is in the world but is not of the world. In the setting of the Christian congregation, then, the demand for peacemaking and the avoidance of violence are inescapable. The church must, of course, do what it can to stem and restrain violence in the larger world. But first and foremost, the church must be what its Master called it to be: a peaceable kingdom, a community where forgiveness and forbearance and mutual regard rule out violence and prepare people to live in the public world as peacemakers who reject acts of violence, even those organized and legitimized by the state.[2]

DEVELOPMENTS IN CHRISTIAN ATTITUDES TOWARD WAR

So long as the church was a tiny minority in the ancient Roman world, no need arose for guidelines as to the exercise of power in

1. See James W. Douglass, *The Nonviolent Coming of God* (Maryknoll, N.Y.: Orbis, 1991).

2. For a forceful presentation of this viewpoint, see Stanley Hauerwas, *The Peaceable Kingdom: A Primer in Christian Ethics* (Notre Dame: University of Notre Dame Press, 1983); and Stanley Hauerwas and William H. Willimon, *Resident Aliens* (Nashville: Abingdon Press, 1989).

times of war. The church was more often than not the victim of Roman political, military, and economic power rather than an actor on the public scene. But with the spread of Christianity and with its public standing as the religion of the Roman Empire (late 4th century C.E.), the situation changed markedly. Bishops had already become arbiters in civil administration, and that responsibility was to grow. The church had the responsibility for offering moral guidance to the empire, and that responsibility was not shirked.

On the basis both of natural law (developed in Greek and Roman political thought even prior to Christianity) and of Christian teaching, there evolved over many centuries the theory of the "just war," as Rabbi Falk has noted. The church came to recognize that wars were indeed going to be waged among nations and tribes, and it sought to offer controls and sanctions in the face of such conflicts. Two sets of guidelines developed, the first for arriving at the decision that a war was indeed justifiable,[3] and the second for assuring that the actual conduct of the war lay within tolerable bounds. Both of these guidelines continue to have value; indeed, as wars tend to be "little" ones rather than massive engagements of the sort seen in the First and Second World Wars, such guidelines are even more useful today than they were in addressing the worldwide conflicts of the first half of this century.

When is war justifiable, on the basis of "just war" theory? When four conditions obtain: One side persists in acts of injustice; the perpetrator cannot be restrained in any other way; there is a sensible proportion between the seriousness of the crimes being committed and the damage that war will do to stop the crimes; and there is a reasonable hope of success. One can see right away that such guidelines might well have been studiously applied, for example, prior to the efforts in Somalia or in the former Yugoslavia to bring peace to the warring peoples and tribes.

How must warfare be conducted, according to "just war" theory? The war must be waged in such a way as to maintain respect for human life, which means that the taking of human life must occur in acts of lawful self-defense. It must be conducted in such fashion

---

3. Thomas Aquinas would later insist that no war was fully just, even though it might be necessary for the Christian and the state to engage in warfare for the sake of justice.

as to demonstrate respect for the selfhood and the humanity of the enemy, which means that torture, rape, and other such acts are ruled out. The war must be waged in such a way as to keep clear the distinction between combatants and the civilian population; only military targets are to be attacked. And in general, all intrinsically evil acts are to be avoided (torture, rape, plunder, medical experimentation, and, above all, elimination of population groups wholesale, as in Nazi Germany). Again, it is easy to see the value of such guidelines as we think of recent engagements in warfare. One reason why Christians were so reluctant to go along with the United States engagement in Iraq was that such tests seemed not to have been met, either in the decision to go to war or (and especially) in the actual conduct of the war. Were all the available means exhausted prior to the decision to go to war? Civilian targets were bombed again and again, and the disproportion in the means of warfare seemed grotesque, as Coalition forces' bombs fell by the tens of thousands upon military targets with no defense whatsoever. The humanity of the Iraqi people seemed to be ignored, with Saddam Hussein demonized by war propaganda. Nonetheless, the difference in the Christian and Jewish perspectives should not be overstated, for many Christians also looked upon the missile attacks on Israel by Iraq as warranting the most extreme measure available against Iraq to stop such assaults upon the civilian population of Israel that went on night after night.

With the advent of nuclear warfare, some have claimed that war as such has become obsolete and impossible to wage on any rational basis at all. Recent history suggests otherwise; the horror of nuclear warfare may be serving as a useful deterrent against the infliction of such horrors again, even though nuclear disarmament clearly is desperately and urgently called for. The "little" wars seem likely to continue, certainly until the day when some effective worldwide governmental structures can be put in place to check quickly such skirmishes when they occur.

It seems possible to argue that Christianity through the centuries has offered some restraints on the conduct of warfare, even though so-called Christian nations have been notoriously ready to go to war against one another, as is the case today. One of those restraints, clearly, has been the inner struggle of the church to deal with the question of whether absolute pacifism is the only authentic Christian position or whether (as noted above) some wars can be justified on the basis of the need to resist injustice and evil.

ORGANIZED CHRISTIAN PACIFISM

In southeastern France and northwestern Italy there arose the earliest major force against any form of Christian engagement in war. The movement developed from the action and teaching of Peter (Pierre) Valdes in 1170, who, as a Christian, refused to engage in warfare and became the leader of the Waldensians, a Christian community that is still strong today throughout Italy and in parts of France and Switzerland. Hussites, Lollards, Moravians, and especially the Anabaptists were to follow, all in their particular ways unwilling to engage in warfare because of Christian conviction. As noted above, some of these groups took the position that to engage in the work of governance at all—as magistrates, for example—was inappropriate for the Christian community, which was to be in the world but not caught up in its acts of governance, acts that could not help involving the Christian in violence against a neighbor.

The best known of the Christian pacifists trace their origin to George Fox, the founder of the Society of Friends, the Quakers. Since the mid-seventeenth century, Quakers have developed their witness to peacemaking and nonviolence in ways that have contributed markedly to the Christian pacifist movement in all the churches.

Since 1914 the Fellowship of Reconciliation has been the major ecumenical Christian body opposing warfare; its members have been ready to pay the price for their pacifism, a price that has included imprisonment and the disdain of Christians and other neighbors on many occasions. The best known of their leaders, A. J. Muste, became a household name during the period between the two World Wars. His influence was still great into the period after the end of the Second World War.

Christian pacifism took a fresh turn in the era of the Vietnam war. Many Christians joined other United States citizens in refusing to serve in the armed forces, because of their conviction that this particular war simply could not be justified on any grounds. The price was often higher for such persons. Alternative forms of public service would be allowed for persons whose religious convictions could be stated along the lines developed by the "Peace Churches." But Vietnam war protesters often took no such position. They were not pacifists—certainly not Christian pacifists of the classical sort—and they did not claim to be. They were protesting a war that should never have been engaged, and much seems today to support the soundness of their position. Such a "selective" pacifism, however, has not been easy for classic Christian pacifism to accept unqualifiedly.

The reason why is clear. Christian pacifism of the Quaker and Mennonite sort has always been accompanied by efforts at peacemaking. The "Peace Churches" do not simply refuse to engage in acts of violence in times of war. They are peacemakers, advocates of arbitration and the settling of conflicts by peaceful means. Mennonite and Quaker groups are among the leaders worldwide in the provision of aid to those in need. They work to resolve conflicts in dozens of lands at the present time. Their commitment to public justice and to the public good is unmistakable, even if they insist that they cannot personally act violently to stem violence.

AN ASSESSMENT OF CHRISTIAN PACIFISM

A faithful Christian witness is always to be commended, even if one can detect what appear to be weaknesses in the witness being borne. In the case of Christian pacifism in its many forms, the strengths are massive and the limitations, as I discern them, are both understandable and perhaps a function of the strengths. We have noted above that there are forms of Christian pacifism that one must reject, or at least call into serious question. Those forms are basically two in number: the pacifism that simply rejects any responsibility for the public world at all, secure in the confidence that God will care for the world in God's own time and way, and the pacifism that pragmatically rejects all efforts on the part of the organized Christian community to offer moral guidance for public life in terms other than narrow Christian theological terms. Contemporary Christian pacifists rarely fall into either error, but the rhetoric of some theologians who adopt what they call a Christian pacifist position seems to lean in the second direction. To the extent that such theologians are actually calling the church to be itself, distinguishable in the world as a community committed to the struggle for peace with justice, the position is to be strongly commended. But if, as it seems to me probable, some such voices are expressing hostility for the contemporary social world and its struggles, the position is to be rejected. It is to be rejected because it is less interested in a strict Christian pacifism than it is in identifying the heresy of other Christians who are struggling, in their way and in their witness, for peace with justice through vigorous engagement with the world's struggles and pains and joys and successes.

The major contribution of Christian pacifism is not difficult to identify. It is the unrelenting effort to call both church and world to break the circle of violence that has been characteristic of human life since its appearance on the earth—so far as we can determine. Already in Genesis 1–11, ancient narratives tell how suspicion and hostility within the human family, born in part at least out of personal anxiety and the instinct for self-preservation, break out and damage life in community as God has established and ordained it. Cain is jealous of his brother Abel because the brother's sacrifice seems to be more acceptable to the deity than Cain's own sacrifice. Not even God's personal counsel and admonitions can assuage this jealousy and the rage that builds up, and we have the first biblical murder. We also see, at the same time, that God will not let violence simply continue. Cain receives God's protective sign so that he is able to live on, damaged and lonely though his life is said to have been.

The spread of violence is met by divine violence to stem it. The massive flood that destroys all life on the planet strikes horror into the hearts of hearers and readers, ancient and contemporary. The preservation of one family from which a new world is born is a sign both of divine grace and determination to maintain life and of divine insistence that violence cannot spread and spread and spread without dreadful consequences. *God will have a blessed and peaceable human community.*

Christian pacifists insist on the same thing. They are ready to risk everything, confident that God demands that *they*, at least, not contribute directly to the continuation and the spread of violence. How can violence ever be stemmed if it is not challenged head-on by some members of the human community at least? It is hard to imagine just how violent our contemporary world would be without the witness of Christian and other pacifists against all forms of violence.

Some may ask whether such an assessment gives too much credit to Christian pacifism. I believe that it does not. The majority position of Christian pacifists is just that sketched. They do not necessarily deny that Christians who reject or question the pacifist position are faithless; they simply insist that, for them, there is no other Christian way. They do not simply leave the world to the devil or to God while they cultivate their own effort to live a pure spiritual life. Rather, they struggle for justice, engage in acts of conciliation and reconciliation, generously give themselves to meeting human need, and accept the state's provision of alternative forms of service in times of warfare.

A good parallel to Christian pacifists from ancient Israel is the life of the Nazirites, those who are committed to a lifelong refusal to join in the culture of Canaan, drinking wine or strong drink, dressing their hair in Canaanite fashion, and otherwise taking up the life of Canaan. The very existence of these "different" Israelites was often a challenge and an affront to the majority population of Israel, as we can see from Amos 2:11-12. In our day, Quakers, Mennonites, and other Christian pacifists often make the rest of the Christian community similarly uncomfortable. It is their very virtue, their goodness, their refusal to compromise—as the rest of us find ourselves drawn to do—that makes the presence of such groups both praiseworthy and an embarrassment.

THE CASE FOR A NONABSOLUTIST CHRISTIAN PACIFISM

The argument here is that the Christian's commitment to active peacemaking and to the settlement of disputes—personal, group, and national—by nonviolent means is a fixed and firm commitment. Acts of violence of any sort, including warfare, should never be called right and just. They should be resorted to only when the alternative would itself be a violation of one's Christian commitment to seek justice and peace. When violence can be stemmed by no other means than violence, then both the Christian community and the larger human community have failed. Resorting to violence is, in and of itself, an acknowledgment of that failure.

It would, however, be a greater moral failure if the entire community of Christians should fail to act in a situation like that created by Adolf Hitler and Nazi Germany. It would not have been a sufficient response to evil of such magnitude for the Christian community to deplore the action, to protest nonviolently, to suffer martyrdom, but to refuse to call for all necessary means to bring an end to such violence. Therein lies the tragic human consequence of accumulated moral evil in the world: The community can reach a point at which past human failings, along with all the fine human achievements, provide a context in which rampant evil breaks out and can only be stemmed by violent acts to stop the violence.

The majority Christian position seems to be along these lines. The Christian is by commitment pacifist, committed to nonviolence in all human relations, unwilling simply to take up arms in time of warfare because the nation calls one to do so. But the Christian is well aware that he or she has responsibility for others, for those suffering oppression and endangerment of life in particular, and must come to their aid by all possible means. Evil in one's own heart and evil in the world must be challenged, stemmed, and, when possible, eradicated. While God alone forgives sin, God's creatures, charged to care for the earth, to pursue justice, and to relieve oppression, must resist evil and, when possible, stop its destruction of human life.

The Christian community has another resource, its greatest resource of all. It has a vision of what God purposes for human life on the planet, a vision shared with the Jewish community as well— where in fact the vision originated. This vision, the moral import of which we will discuss more fully in our last chapter, is what binds together both the absolute Christian pacifist and the non-absolute Christian pacifist. All Christians, I would maintain, share this vision of *God's own commitment to peace with justice in a renewed universe*. The promise by Israel's prophets of a time when human beings, Jew and Gentile alike, would live together in peace, sharing the goods of earth, practicing justice, and supporting one another on God's transformed earth, is one of the great testimonies of the Bible. The promise is reaffirmed in the Christian community; indeed, the Christian community makes the bold claim that within the band of Christian believers this promised "kingdom of God" is already finding realization. And what is finding realization within the inner life of the Christian community, the church, is also spreading out to touch the whole of life—public and private, economic and political.

The Christian commitment to peace and justice and to nonviolent means of settling disputes and problems is a commitment that is nurtured by Christian worship, by life together that draws on the power of the Holy Spirit for continuing renewal and transformation of life, and by mutual correction and support. Christian peacemaking needs the continuing refreshment, renewal, and recommitment that come from the life of faith with one's co-believers. It is nurtured in a special way, I would contend, by the community's vision of God's world of righteousness and peace that God is bringing to earth. Let me try to show how, though elaboration is to come in the final chapter.

Hope in God's Coming Rule Brings Judgment Upon the Community

The community can never be content with a merely tolerable peace. If God is bringing peace with righteousness to earth, and is doing so through the community of Christian faith, then that community is under divine mandate and judgment to struggle for peace day by day, year by year, never content with anything less than what God is committed to bring and is indeed bringing even now. Since this vision is of the world made peaceable and righteous, it is not enough for the local congregation to be just and peaceable; the community within which it lives must also be. So long as it is not, and that of course seems to be always the case, the community has not yet done its part and is under judgment to try and try again. Warfare, in this view and in the light of this Christian vision, is not only unjust, but it is also in flat contradiction with what God is bringing to earth.

Hope in God's Coming Rule Provides Confidence

At the same time, the community of faith holds firmly to the belief that God is in fact the great peacemaker and establisher of justice and that God is working even now for both—through the Christian community and also apart from that community. The struggle for peace with righteousness, then, which seems never to succeed, is not futile. The community cannot allow itself to believe that the struggle is futile or pointless, for that would be to give the lie to God's promise of a transformed earth that is even now underway. So there is always hope.

Hope in God's Coming Rule Impels Us Forward

Moreover, the confidence we have in the coming of God's peace with righteousness is more than confidence; it is a vision that is renewed over and over again within the community of faith as signs of its truth and power show up both within that community of faith and beyond its boundaries. The vision draws us forward, buoyed up by our actual experience of peacemaking that works, of righteousness that stands forth in an unrighteous and evil world, of transforming love and joy that are not merely personal and inward but a part of the very fabric of community life.

THE VALUE OF NONABSOLUTIST CHRISTIAN PACIFISM

The weight and value of this Christian position are evident, I believe. The commitment is always to public righteousness and peace, to the settling of conflicts apart from and without violence and forceful intervention and intimidation. But the very commitment to the Christian vision of God's coming rule on earth is a reminder that the Christian community cannot let the structures of peace with righteousness that God is bringing to earth go unattended and despised. While the presence of absolute pacifists within the Christian community is a boon and a blessing of incalculable worth and strength, the Christian community as a whole must be continuously attentive to opportunities to shore up and strengthen what, in faith, we affirm to be God's own work in the world. We cannot be silent when violence tears a community apart, as it does today in so many parts of our world. Active efforts toward peacemaking, by nonviolent means if at all possible, are a part of the Christian mandate to "be fruitful and multiply, and fill the earth and subdue it" (Gen. 1:28). But when all else fails and God's own world of peace with righteousness is under continuing assault, the Chris-

107

tian community has the moral obligation to cry out before the public authorities, as did the widow to the judge (Luke 18:1-8), "Give us justice! Stop this injustice!"

But how is the individual Christian member to take up this mandate to maintain and further the work that God is doing for justice and peace in the world? On the basis of lively and continuing debate and prayer and consensus building within the believing congregation, never despising the judgments of those with whom one does not agree, but finally holding fast to the disclosure of what God will have each individual do. Here, as we can see, there will be differences within the community, time after time.

Church bodies and denominations will have their different ways of acting in the face of such differences of judgment. Religious liberty, as we saw above, safeguards that church bodies not make the mistake of identifying their understanding of the divine will with the decisions taken by a secular state. But Christian bodies, individual and national and worldwide, as well as individual Christian citizens, should be prepared to labor through their governments for the spread of what they are convinced in faith is the path that leads most closely toward God's own work in behalf of peace with righteousness for the whole world.

SUGGESTED READING

Augsburger, Myron S. *Nuclear Arms: Two Views on World Peace.* Waco, Tex.: Word Press, 1987.

Burggraeve, Roger. *Swords into Plowshares: Theological Reflections on Peace.* Louvain: Peeters Press, 1991.

The Cross and the Bomb: Christian Ethics and the Nuclear Debate. London: Mowbray, 1983.

Johnson, James Turner, *Can Modern War Be Just?* New Haven, Conn.: Yale University Press, 1984.

Kelsay, John. *Islam and War: A Study in Comparative Ethics.* Louisville: Westminster Press, 1993.

Peace, Politics, and the People of God. Philadelphia: Fortress Press, 1986.

Shannon, Thomas A. *What Are They Saying About Peace and War?* Maryknoll, N.Y.: Orbis, 1983

Studying War No More? From Just War to Just Peace. Grand Rapids, Mich.: Eerdmans, 1994.

Vanderhaar, Gerard A. *Active Non-Violence: A Way of Personal Peace.* Mystic, Conn.: Twenty-third Publications, 1990.

A CHRISTIAN OUTLOOK

Yoder, John Howard. *Nevertheless: The Varieties and Shortcomings of Religious Pacifism*. Scottdale, Pa.: Herald Press, 1992.
Yoder, Perry B., and William M. Swartley, eds. *The Meaning of Peace: Biblical Studies*. Louisville: Westminster/John Knox Press, 1992.

CHAPTER FIVE

JEWS, CHRISTIANS, AND MUSLIMS

PREFACE

There may be a question as to why a chapter on Jews, Christians, and Muslims should be included in a book entitled *Jews and Christians: In Pursuit of Social Justice*. The answer is that with the rapid growth of the Muslim community in the United States and throughout the world, it is urgent that lines of communication be opened among these three major Western religions.

Jews and Christians know far too little about Muslim beliefs and practices. By the same token, most Muslims have little knowledge of Judaism and Christianity. We need to educate each other. Moreover, once we have come to know and understand each other, we must focus on those areas of mutual concern that together we can address. The social issues in which we see moral challenges for all three faiths provide an opportunity for us to join hands in the pursuit of freedom and justice for all people.

This chapter, then, will seek to provide insights into the historical background for our relationship, as well as similarities and differences in our theology and our way of life. We hope it will encourage Jews and Christians to reach out to our Muslim neighbors for helpful dialogue and for affirmation of the religious commitments that are the great heritage we share.

JEWS, CHRISTIANS, AND MUSLIMS

A JEWISH OUTLOOK

Jews and Muslims share much in common, historically and theologically. They are unique, in that of all the world religions, these are the only ones that incorporate both a religious commitment and a strong nationalism in the foundations of their traditions. In the religious aspects of Judaism and Islam there is a fundamental agreement in the belief in one God. The two religions share many other theological beliefs, though there are also conflicts, especially in their relationships to Muhammed, the final prophet of Islam, and in the rivalries of their missionary outreach. Far more difficult, however, has been the nationalistic aspirations of Jews and Muslims, especially in their claims to be the rightful possessors of Palestine. Both peoples have been affected by the radical extremists, on the one hand, who would brook no compromise in their claims to the land and, on the other hand, by those more moderate voices who have sought and continue to seek a common ground on which Jews and Muslims can live together in peace. The history of these peoples, therefore, is highlighted both by periods of mutual respect through shared beliefs and by periods of bitter conflict and hostility.

We begin in the sixth and seventh centuries of the common era, when a number of Jewish tribes had settled in Arabia living side by side, sometimes at peace, often in conflict, with the more numerous Arab tribes. Those Jews were rivals with early Christians in their missionary endeavors to convert the Arabs to their respective faiths. Both groups enjoyed success in their proselytizing, and large numbers of Arabs became familiar with both Hebrew Scriptures and the New Testament. It is understandable, therefore, that Muhammed was attracted to many rituals and doctrines in Judaism and sought to develop his own religion for the Arab world, to be joined, he hoped, by the Jews in proclaiming a universal faith.

The basic tenet that Muhammed shared with Judaism was the belief in one God. When he began his teaching in Mecca, Muhammed was surrounded by Arab idolators, and he sought to bring them a belief in one God and an appreciation of the highest moral tenets of Judaism. Waraka Ibn-Naufal, a cousin of Chadija, Muhammed's wife, had converted to Judaism and knew Hebrew well; he also imbued Muhammed with a love for the religion of Abraham. Muhammed's first teachings, therefore, were strongly influenced by Jewish beliefs and practices. He communicated this to his friends and followers. First and foremost he proclaimed the same fundamental principle as in Judaism: "There is no God but Allah," and only much later added, as an integral part of this confession of faith, "and Muhammed is his prophet."

When Muhammed found that the Arab idolators in Mecca were not receptive to his teachings, and even threatened his life, he moved to Medina in 622 C.E., where he was favorably received by numerous Jews, who thought that Muhammed's goal was to bring the Arab world to an acceptance of Judaism. Muhammed employed a Jewish scribe for many years, and it is thought that through this scribe and other learned Jews, Muhammed became familiar with the Mosaic Revelation with which the Koran Revelation agreed in essence.

The profound influence of Judaism in the early development of Islam can be appreciated in these basic teachings in Muhammed's early work:

1. The belief in Allah as the only true God and the negation of all other gods that were revered in Arabia (for the Jewish parallel, see Deut. 6:4).
2. The revelation of a written law that was handed down to Muhammed from the heavenly *Umm al-Kitab* (the original scripture) by the angel Gabriel. (For the Jewish parallel, see the giving of the Law to Moses by God in Exodus 20 and Deuteronomy 5, and the Orthodox Jewish doctrine that teaches that all of Torah was revealed by God to Moses at Sinai).
3. The introduction of the concept of the Day of Judgment, resulting in the assumption by Islam of a moral character (see eschatology in the book of Ezekiel in Hebrew Scriptures).

4. The hallowing of the personality of Abraham, "the Merciful Friend," as the first to profess monotheism (see Genesis 12).
5. The introduction of religious laws in which there is evidence of moral and social progress in comparison to the situation preceding Muhammed's appearance (compare with the teachings of the Hebrew prophets).
6. The laying of the foundations for the religious and political organization of his believers that abolished the tribal regime and first endowed Islam with its double character of both religion and state (a clear parallel with Judaism's double character).
7. The laying down of the Arabic language as the religious language of Islam (compare to Hebrew as the sacred language of Judaism).

Throughout his lifetime, Muhammed recognized the influence of Judaism on Islam. He felt that he was reviving and purifying the ancient religion. It was only when he recognized in Medina that the Jews did not accept Islam as the Arab version of their religion, and therefore were not embracing Islam, that Muhammed began to develop distinctions between Islam and Judaism. These were the initial changes Muhammed made to distinguish between the two faiths:

1. The direction in which prayers were to be recited would no longer follow the Jewish custom of facing toward Jerusalem in prayer. Muslims would henceforth turn toward Mecca.
2. He abolished the fast of the tenth day of the month of Muharram, which had paralleled the Jewish fast day of Yom Kippur, and replaced it by the fast of the month of Ramadan.
3. Friday replaced the Jewish Saturday as the Sabbath for Islam, and the prohibition of work on the Sabbath, which was basic to Jewish observance, was lifted, except during midday prayer.
4. The Jewish custom of praying three times a day was replaced by Muslims' being required to face Mecca and pray five times daily.
5. Muhammed was very lenient in regard to the Jewish dietary laws. The major prohibitions against eating pork, the blood of animals, and animals not slaughtered with the invocation of Allah, however, were maintained.

None of this, however, changed the general character of the religious beliefs Islam shared with Judaism.

The early anti-Jewish religious prejudices in Islam resulted, to a great extent, from the Koran. In the revelations of the Koran, however, we find praise of the Jews and Judaism. Two passages from Sura II ("The Cow") serve to illustrate the positive attitude of the Koran in relationship to Jews:

> "Children of Israel, remember My blessing wherewith I blessed you,
> and that I have preferred you above all beings."[1]
> "And they say, 'Be Jews or Christians and
> you shall be guided.' Say thou: 'Nay rather
> the creed of Abraham, a man of pure faith;
>   he was no idolator.'
> Say you: 'We believe in God, and in that
> which was sent down on us and sent down on
> Abraham, Ishmael, Isaac and Jacob, and the
> Tribes, and that which was given to Moses
> and Jesus and the Prophets, of their Lord;
> we make no division between any of them, and
>   to Him we surrender.' "[2]

In other Suras we see the antagonism toward Jews who have not accepted Islam, and which later became a basis for persecution of Jews by Muslims. One example is from Sura IV ("Women"):

> Some of the Jews pervert words from their
> meanings saying, "We have heard and we disobey"
> and "Hear, and be thou not given to hear"
> and "Observe us," twisting with their tongues
>   and traducing religion.[3]

Another from Sura V (The Table):

> O believers, take not Jews and Christians
> as friends; they are friends of each other.
> Whoso of you makes them his friends
> is one of them. God guides not the people
>   of the evildoers.[4]

1. A. Arberry, *The Koran Interpreted* (New York: Macmillan, 1955), 34.
2. Ibid., 45.
3. Ibid., 107.
4. Ibid., 136.

Finally, from Sura IX ("Repentance"):

The Jews say, "Ezra is the Son of God";
That is the utterance of their mouths, conforming
with the unbelievers before them. God assail
    them! How they are perverted!
They have taken their rabbis and their monks as
    Lords apart from God.[5]

The other religious basis for anti-Semitism among many Muslims goes back to both Jewish and Muslim claims of Abraham as their first patriarch. Jews trace their relationship to Abraham through Isaac, while Muslims trace theirs through Ishmael. Many Orthodox Muslims, to this day, maintain that the covenant of God's land, given to Abraham, should have been inherited by Ishmael, since he was Abraham's firstborn and, therefore, was entitled to inherit that promised land (Palestine). Jews, on the other hand, maintain that since Ishmael was the son of the concubine, Hagar, and since Isaac was Abraham's firstborn to his wife, Sarah, Isaac is the rightful claimant to be inheritor of the convenanted land. Jews, furthermore, point to God's promise in the book of Genesis that Ishmael will be the father of another nation in another land, and that Isaac will be Abraham's successor, as the basis for their claim to the promised land. This conflict is still the cause celebre that many orthodox Muslims use for inciting their followers to join in a holy war (a jihad) against Israel.

Religious controversy between these two major Western religions continued into the Middle Ages. It was highlighted by the forced conversion to Islam of the messianic pretender Sabbatai Zevi in the seventeenth century. Zevi had gained a considerable following among Jews and some Muslims who believed that he was the promised Messiah. In England, Poland, Holland, and Spain his following continued to increase. Sabbatai Zevi's incursion into Muslim ranks became a deep concern of the sultan Mahomet IV. Vanni, a proselytizing cleric, suggested that an attempt be made to bring Sabbatai over to Islam. This advice was followed, and the sultan's physician, a Jew by the name of Guidon, was employed as the

5. Ibid., 210.

medium. The physician represented to Sabbatai the dreadful punshment that would befall him if he did not convert to Islam: He would be bound and scourged through the streets with burning torches, if he did not appease the sultan by adopting Islam. The next day he was brought before the sultan and immediately cast off his Jewish headdress. He accepted a white Turkish turban and a green mantle, and so his conversion was completed. Some of Sabbatai's followers converted with him, but the vast majority repudiated his messianic pretensions and denounced him as a traitor. This created severe tensions between the sultan and the Jewish community. Grave punishments of chief rabbis and their followers were threatened, but fortunately were never carried out.[6]

The experience of Jews under Islam varied widely in different periods of history and under Muslim leaders who ranged in their religious doctrines from ultra orthodox to liberal. The common areas of conflict centered around the refusal of the Jews to accept Muhammed as God's prophet, forced conversions of Jews by Muslims throughout history, and the insistent claim by both religions of the right to control Jerusalem as a sacred center of religious heritage. However, the emerging Islamic faith shared most of Judaism's religious practices and theological themes. In addition to those beliefs and practices already noted, the most striking parallel in Judaism and Islam is found in the system of religious law, divine regulations of the minute matters of morality and custom in everyday life. The law is the core of both religions. These bodies of law, the Talmud in Judaism and Sharia in Islam, are collections of answers by religious leaders and scholars to questions posed on matters of ethics, Sabbath and holiday observances, family life, and the like. The Islamic religious law seems to have grown directly out of the Talmud. Study of the law is considered a part of worship by Jews and Muslims. Each religion currently has religious courts in Jerusalem to adjudicate disputes and to administer the translation of the oral tradition into practical living. Although there are many contrasts within the two bodies of law, as, for example, in rules of inheritance, many of the laws are similar.

Rabbi David Hartman, a widely respected Orthodox leader in

6. H. Graetz, *History of the Jews*, vols. II, IV, V (Philadelphia: The Jewish Publication Society, 1967), 5:154-55.

Israel, has observed that "Islam is much closer to Judaism than to Christianity. There is much more sense of the transcendant God, the non-image God, the imageless God. Its tremendous concern with law. Law and theology are much closer. And the place that the community plays in spiritual life, and on a cultural level, the family, the role of the family, are all ways in which we can be talking to each other."[7]

Just as we have seen that Islam drew much from Judaism, so Judaism also felt the impact of Islam. From earliest times, through the medieval period, up to the modern period, as Jews scattered throughout the Diaspora, the finest Jewish life and culture were found in Muslim lands. One of the most interesting areas of Judeo-Islamic interaction was in the practice of travel for religious study or pilgrimage. J. D. Goitein has observed that "journeys whose aim was a visit to famous scholars and schools were an old Jewish custom, most conspicuous in talmudic literature, and this tradition received new impetus under Arab rule, where travel for study's sake became a characteristic aspect of Muslim civilization. As a visit to Mecca or another holy place became an obligation for a Muslim at least once in his lifetime, so a Jew living in Spain or North Africa in the eighth or ninth century, would aspire to behold Jerusalem before he died."[8]

The finest example of one of the most illustrious thinkers in Jewish history who was profoundly influenced by Islam is Moses ben Maimon, known better as Maimonides. It has been said of him "from Moses (the great Law-giver) to Moses (ben Maimon), there was none like unto Moses." He was a physician, astronomer, philosopher, and religious scholar. Born in Cordoba, Spain in the twelfth century, he spent most of his life in Cairo, Egypt. In both countries, he was physician to the court. He lived and wrote in the Golden Age of Spain, during which Jewish culture and religion flourished under Islamic rule. Maimonides' major philosophic work, "Guide of the Perplexed," took as its central theme that life's only worthwhile purpose is pure, abstract thinking on Greek philosophy as interpreted by Islam. Goitein observes that "the *Guide of the Perplexed* is a great monument of Jewish-Arab symbiosis, not merely because it is

7. D. Shipler, *Arab and Jew: Wounded Spirits in a Promised Land* (New York: Times Books, 1986), 363.
8. Ibid.

written in Arabic by an original Jewish thinker and was studied by Arabs, but because it developed and conveyed to large sections of the Jewish people ideas which had so long occupied the Arab mind."[9]

Hartman also sees in Maimonides' writing a basis for Judeo-Islamic accord: "Maimonides wrote a major response about Islam not being paganism, and had a very high regard for Islamic monotheism. So there is a very, very interesting tradition in which the Jewish philosopher, Maimonides, the greatest Jewish Halakhist-philosopher of Jewish history, lives with intense dialogue and respect for Islamic philosophy. So there is a precedent now for a rich intercultural, spiritual theme. There is enormous ground on which that could be possible."[10]

It would be fair to say that Jews, along with other minorities in Muslim countries, enjoyed a degree of freedom to practice their religions, though they were forced to pay a poll tax for that privilege and to endure certain other disabilities. Jewish religion and culture flourished in most Muslim lands, though there were also periods of intense proselytization when more fanatic Muslims sought converts at the point of a sword. The major conflicts between Muslims and Jews developed around political issues, primarily concerning control of Jerusalem and of the "holy land." The history of these warring nationalisms is too long and too complex to be covered in detail in this chapter. It is important, nevertheless, to attempt an understanding of the tragic conflict between these two peoples.

The twentieth-century tensions began toward the end of the First World War when the British government issued the famous Balfour Declaration, which stated basically that Britain's government viewed with favor the establishment in Palestine of a Jewish state. This was a great victory for the fledgling Zionist movement, and it was a bitter and totally unacceptable loss for the Muslim world. Shortly thereafter the League of Nations made Great Britain the mandatory power to solve the Palestinian problem. Britain's attempt to govern Palestine and mediate the conflicts between Jews and Muslims was a tragic failure. The mandate ended with the demise

9. Ibid., 367.
10. Ibid.

of the League of Nations, and the Palestine question had found no solutions.

Following the conclusion of the Second World War, the newly established United Nations appointed still another commission to investigate the problems and to formulate a solution. Eventually the commission presented to the United Nations its Partition Plan, which divided Palestine into a Jewish state and an Arab state, with a majority Jewish population in one and a majority of Arabs in the other. The plan was not satisfactory to either party, but the Jewish leaders were convinced that this was the best that could be expected at the time, and so accepted the U.N. plan; the state of Israel was born in 1948. The surrounding Arab states refused to accept the U.N. plan and immediately declared war on the Jewish state. Miraculously the state of Israel, without any aid from other countries, survived the invasion of the five Arab states, and succeeded in driving the invaders from the newly formed state. For almost twenty years Israel and the Arab states lived with an armed truce. Then, in 1967, the surrounding Arab states once again invaded Israel. This time, not only did Israel repulse the invaders in six days, but also expanded the original land allotted it by the U.N. to include for the first time a united Jerusalem and defensible borders with Jordan, Egypt, Lebanon, and Syria. Again the Arab states refused to agree to a peace treaty with Israel; but with the capture of the Golan Heights from Syria, the Sinai desert from Egypt, and the West Bank, including old Jerusalem and the Gaza Strip from Jordan, Israel's military defense was much more secure.

This truce was shortlived, however, and in 1973 Egypt and Syria led the Arabs in another invasion of Israel in what became known as the Yom Kippur War. Again Israel successfully repelled the invaders, though with heavy losses in life and property. Each war and each defeat increased the bitterness of the Arab world and the resultant virulent anti-Semitism. Saudi Arabia published especially vicious attacks on Judaism. One paper carried an article headlined "The Torah as the Source of Jewish War Crimes," which began, "People who do not read the Torah and are not experts in it wonderingly ask about the love of destruction and the will to exterminate that characterize Zionism." It declared, "The Jewish religion is nothing but a collection of criminal racist principles, sowing cruelty, blood-lust, and killing in those who believe in it." And the Saudi daily *Al-Riyad* declared, "The Talmud and its writings maintain that the world is the property of God's people, the chosen, because the members of the human race are slaves to them. . . . These abominable ideas have led the Jews in the course of history to adventurism, espionage, and usury."[11]

Egyptian publications were less virulent in their attacks in the 1970s and during the peace process that began in 1977, but the assaults resumed shortly thereafter. At the 1981 Cairo Book Fair, these titles appeared on the shelves: *The Jews: Objects of the Wrath of God* and *The War of Survival Between the Koran and the Talmud.* In the fourth edition of *The Wailing Wall and the Tears,* the editor asserts that the Talmud urges Jews to kill non-Jews. *Jews, History and Doctrine* by Kamil Safan revives the blood libel circulated in Damascus in which Jews were accused of killing non-Jewish children to use their blood for making matzot during Passover.[12] Similar examples of anti-Semitic diatribes can be found in publications in Syria, Lebanon, and Iran.

It is pointless to attempt to refute all of these accusations here. Any fair-minded student of Judaism and Jewish history knows that these charges are baseless.

The first cause for hope in Jewish-Arab relations came with the Camp David accord, signed by Sadat of Egypt and Begin of Israel, under the leadership of U.S. President Jimmy Carter. This agreement was followed by a visit to Jerusalem by Sadat. The treaty essentially provided that Israel return to Egypt the entire Sinai Peninsula, captured during the Six Day War, in return for Egypt's pledge not to start a war with Israel. More recently, an accord between Israel and Jordan has paved the way for Israel's negotiating with the Palestinians to enter into the first phases of establishing some measure of independence for the Palestinians on the West Bank and in the Gaza Strip, leading eventually, it is to be hoped, to the establishment of an independent Palestinian state.

The problems surrounding this important step toward peace between Arabs and Israelis are manifold. To some extent, the barriers to peace between the Arab states and the state of Israel mirror

11. Ibid., 174.
12. Ibid., 174-75.

the conflicts that also exist between the Arab nations and the nations of Western Europe and the United States. Most crucial is the necessity of the Arab world's coming to terms with democracy, both within their own countries and in establishing common ground with the Western democracies. Second, the low status of women in Islam poses a very real concern. Judaism and Christianity insist on the equality of the sexes in all aspects of communal life and especially in allowing for normalization of social relationships. Finally, the Muslim world must accept the fact that the ancient call of *jihad* ("holy war") is no longer a viable alternative in achieving Arab aspirations in "the holy land." For the fundamentalist Muslims this matter of *jihad* is probably the most difficult traditional religious doctrine to eliminate from their approach to the "infidel" Jews who have established the state of Israel.

This advocacy of a holy war by fundamentalist Muslim leaders is but one illustration of the difficulties that both Muslims and Israelis encounter in dealing with their nationalist aspirations. The political leadership of both Arab and Israeli nations would be able to work together much more constructively were it not for the religious extremists on both sides. The orthodox Muslims, with a heritage going back to the Crusades in medieval times, will never be satisfied until Jerusalem is under their control and until the "infidel" Jews have been pushed into the sea. By the same token, the Orthodox Rabbis still control the balance of political power in Israel through their small political parties that are needed by the major political parties in order to form a government and maintain a working majority in the Knesset. Since the Orthodox Jews are unwilling to cede to the Palestinians any of the land they believe was promised by God to Abraham and Moses as part of God's covenant with the Jewish people, they are determined to block any agreement that would establish a Palestinian state. Liberal secular and religious leaders and their constituencies on both sides recognize the necessity for compromise regarding the land and other economic and political issues. The great difficulty in establishing positive relationships between Israel and the Arab states is that the orthodox extremists in Israel, in Syria, in Egypt, and in the emerging Palestinian state resort to terrorist activities that keep the Middle East in constant turmoil. Were it not for these extremists, Arabs and Jews would be much

121

closer to finding solutions that would be mutually beneficial in every area of life.

This is not to say that progress has not been made in Arab-Israeli relations. The treaty between Egypt and Israel has held, and there has been no war on their borders. Unfortunately, the fundamentalist Muslims in Egypt have blocked more cultural and social interchange between the two peoples. The agreement between Jordan and Israel will be most important in helping to establish a viable Palestinian state. It is to be hoped that a solution to the tensions between Israel and Syria, focused on control of the Golan Heights, will be found in the near future.

In the meantime, much has been accomplished in bringing about closer ties between Arabs and Jews in academic institutions and in many areas of health and social welfare. Organizations like Interns for Peace have successfully brought Arab and Jewish young people together for a number of successful projects in which the young people live and work together. Through all the years of turmoil, Arabs living in the state of Israel have maintained good relationships with their Jewish neighbors. Members of the Israeli Arab community sit in the Knesset (the Israeli legislature), and most important, the Muslim clerics have the freedom to officiate at their religious services and all their life-cycle events.

Peter Waldeman, writing in the *Wall Street Journal* in March 1995, begins his article on Muslim thinkers reinterpreting Islam for modern times by stating: "There is a famous saying in Islam that 'the gates of innovation' closed 1,000 years ago, sealing the creed forever. The Muslim's duty is to obey, the adage suggests; never to invent. Slowly, however, the gates are opening again."

To illustrate his thesis, Waldeman points out that in Jordan professors at a new Islamic university are assigning student papers on the human rights implications of Islamic law's treatment of women and non-Muslims. In Egypt, Islamic writers are condemning the use of violence by Muslim extremists. Activists in Turkey, Algeria, and Iran are crusading for human rights based on this seldom-heard idea in Muslim teachings: Islam forbids all forms of coercion.

There is also debate today in the Muslim world regarding the Islamic duty of *jihad*. This Arab word, which literally means "struggle," can connote either "holy war" or "personal striving." Such

choices by liberal Muslims in developing contemporary interpretations of Muslim philosophy are predicated on the idea that Islam
today need not adhere to the canons of the tenth century. Underlying
that proposition is the premise that not all Islamic law was ordained
by God. The reformers argue that much of it was adapted by people.
These liberal reformers also insist that violence, even in the name of
God, can never solve modern Islamic problems. Only a regeneration
of Islamic ideas will bring prosperity and peace in their war-torn
sector of the world.

In the United States, many Jewish and Islamic congregations are
holding meetings in cities throughout the country to get to know
each other, to understand their areas of accord as well as areas of
difference. Most significant was a convocation held in Chicago in
March 1995. It was co-sponsored by the Union of American Hebrew
Congregations, the American Muslim Council, the Spertus Institute
of Jewish Studies, and the American Islamic College; both academic
institutions are located in Chicago. The keynote addresses were
presented by Rabbi Alexander Schindler, President of the U.A.H.C.,
and by Imam Warith D. Muhammad, spiritual leader of the largest
African American Muslim group in the U.S.

Rabbi Schindler noted that "we in America, as Muslim and Jew,
are better able to reclaim our common heritage and to engage in a
fruitful dialogue than we are in our father's house. This is the great
tragedy of contemporary life that in ancient Hebron, Muslim and
Jew are still incapable of dialogue or even of peaceful silence. Here,
we are both religious minorities, united in our awareness of the
democratic rights and freedoms that protect us from the homogeniz-
ing desires of a dominant majority. Here the great principle of
separation of church and state secures the sanctity of our religious
autonomy."

Imam Muhammad responded by characterizing Islam as a religion that advocates peace and kindness toward enemies. "Some of
our black spokespersons are hurting us by attacking Jews," he said.
In a passionate denunciation of Black anti-Semitism the Imam cited
the harm that results "when the words or actions of a part of the
community are taken to represent the actions of the whole." Imam
Muhammad also denounced terrorism by Islamic fundamentalist
militants as contrary to Islamic law and teaching. He added that

123

leaders of the Muslim community must stand on the Koran in opposing those who make the innocent the target of their terror. The Imam concluded by saying that there was no problem in recognizing the state of Israel, since "our religion doesn't recognize any human as owner of the land. God is the owner of the earth, and we are trustees."

Just as Jews and Christians have for many years entered into dialogue that we might find the common ground on which we can stand together, so also must Muslims and Jews build on the tentative beginnings of communication and of trust under the leadership of men like Rabbi Schindler and Imam Muhammad. We have much in common that we can share in our histories, our Scriptures, and our basic beliefs. We recognize differences, too, that must be respected and, where possible, reconciled. If Western civilization as we know it is to survive into the twenty-first century, Jews and Christians and Muslims must unite in studying together our common heritage, and then in working together for the establishment of God's kingdom of justice and peace on earth. And together we must respond to the challenge of the Prophet Malachi: "Have we not all one father? Has not one God created us? Why then are we faithless to one another, profaning the covenant of our ancestors?" (Mal. 2:10).

SUGGESTED READING

Arberry, A. *The Koran Interpreted*. New York: Macmillan, 1955.

Encyclopaedia Judaica. Vol. 9. Jerusalem, Israel: Keter Publishing House, 1971.

Graetz, H. *History of the Jews*. Vols. II, IV, V. Philadelphia: The Jewish Publication Society, 1967.

Howe, I., and C. Gershman. *Israel, The Arabs & the Middle East*. New York: Bantam Books, 1972.

Payne, R. *The History of Islam*. New York: Dorset Press, 1990.

Reuther, R., and H. Ruether. *The Wrath of Jonah*. San Francisco: Harper & Row, 1989.

Shipler, D. *Arab and Jew: Wounded Spirits in a Promised Land*. New York: Times Books, 1986.

Spencer, W. *The Islamic States in Conflict*. New York: Franklin Watts, 1983.

The Jewish Encyclopedia. Vol. VI. New York: Funk and Wagnalls Co., 1904.

JEWS, CHRISTIANS, AND MUSLIMS

A CHRISTIAN OUTLOOK

THE SPREAD OF CHRISTIANITY INTO ARABIC-SPEAKING LANDS

Islam and Christianity are related from the time of the birth of Islam. There seems to be no doubt that Christianity had spread into the southwestern corner of the Arabian Peninsula well before the time of Islam. There the prophet Muhammed learned what he knew of Christianity, just as he learned from his even closer association with Jews in the region a good deal about Judaism.

But Christianity in Arabic-speaking lands was much older than Islam; exactly how much older remains obscure. Christians in first-century Palestine would have spoken a number of languages, principally Aramaic, Hebrew, and Greek. But Christianity surely spread south into areas in which Nabatean (the language of the biblical land of Edom and of areas to the south and west) was spoken, and Christian faith spread as well into Egypt, into the Sinai area, and on along the shores of the Red Sea all the way to what is today the Republic of Yemen. There are inscriptions in the Arabic language dating from as early as the fourth century C.E., and the Arabic language had become a literary language soon thereafter, providing Muhammed with the linguistic heritage that he then molded into classical Arabic as found in the Koran. Thus we may assume an Arabic-speaking Christianity in southwest Arabia at least a century or two before the appearance of Islam.

It was in Palestine and in immediately adjacent lands, however, that Arabic Christianity was to take root and flourish. Aramaic-speaking Christians were soon found in what are today the lands of Lebanon, Syria, and Iraq, and Coptic-speaking Christians flourished in Egypt and the Sudan. The liturgies of these Christian groups were long to remain in the traditional languages (Greek, Syriac [which replaced Aramaic in most locations], Coptic, Armenian, and later Ethiopic as well); but by the time of Islam's spread into the Middle East, Arabic became the spoken language and soon became a rival literary language to the liturgical languages of the church. One of the great barriers to a more intimate theological dialogue between Christians and Muslims was the continuing use of these great traditional languages, with their literatures, among the many Christian groups that were adopting Arabic as their native tongue. The Christian groups quite deliberately preferred not to engage in theological discussions with Muslims in Arabic, the language of the Koran, and Muslims soon learned to treasure the classical Arabic of the Koran and sought to reserve its classical terms for use in Islam only.[1]

THE ORIGIN OF ISLAM

Rabbi Falk has traced the origins of Islam and its early connections with Judaism. Christianity, too, was a clear factor in the work of Muhammed. He saw in both Judaism and Christianity the revelation of the one God, unhappily distorted and misunderstood (in his view) by both Jews and Christians. The Koran has many references to Jesus, to Mary, and to John the Baptist, and there are sections of the Koran that clearly indicate that Muhammed was well informed about the stories in the Gospels in particular. Coptic and Ethiopic Christianity have preserved many of the legends of Mary and of Jesus; it is likely that Muhammed's knowledge of the New Testament came from Christians who were familiar with these extra-biblical legends.

Muhammed's chief concern with Christian belief centered on two cardinal Christian theological understandings: Jesus' suffering and death on the cross as an act of faithfulness to God and the Christian doctrine of the Holy Trinity, which (understandably but wrongly) Muhammed took to be a denial of the oneness of God, a cardinal

1. See Kenneth Cragg, *The Arab Christian* (Louisville: Westminster/John Knox, 1991), especially chapter 12.

tenet of Judaism and of Islam.[2] Muhammed held to the view (also held within some Christian circles but declared to be a heresy by the church) that God did not permit the prophet and messenger Jesus to die on the cross. Instead, God provided a substitute who actually died and was buried, while God brought Jesus into heaven to await the general resurrection. And Muhammed sternly rejected the Christian notion of God as three in one, for that seemed to demand belief in three deities: the Creator/Father, the Redeemer/Son, and the Spirit/Guide. I will have more to say later about how these misunderstandings of Christian faith on the part of Muhammed became a fixed part of the conflicts between Muslims and Christians. I will also suggest ways by which both of these misunderstandings might offer the opportunity for a fresh dialogue between contemporary Muslim and Christian theologians.

MUSLIM TREATMENT OF CHRISTIANS IN MUSLIM-CONTROLLED LANDS

Islam made its early gains in southwestern Asia, northeastern Africa, and southeastern Europe through military conquest and the imposition of Islam as the religion of the conquered lands. A special consideration was given, however, to Jews and Christians, since Muhammed looked upon these two religious communities as precursors to Islam, which was bringing to both the definitive truth from the One God. No doubt, Christians suffered severely in many areas of the rapidly expanding Muslim world. And it was not long until the Byzantine Christian forces were engaged in bitter military conflict with the armies of Islam throughout much of the territory of the Holy Roman Empire.

But the armies of Islam seemed invincible. Soon, Islam controlled a vast empire from South Arabia to the borders of India, including the contemporary lands of Afghanistan, Pakistan, Iran, Iraq, Syria,

---

2. See especially Suras 3 and 19. Over and over again, Muhammed makes references to Jesus, to John the Baptist and the vision to his father, Zechariah, and to Mary the mother of Jesus. Muhammed's knowledge is by no means superficial, but it centers more upon these three than upon the broad sweep of Christian history and thought. The apostle Paul, for example, is not of interest to Muhammed.

Jordan, Lebanon, Turkey, Israel (including the West Bank and Gaza), Egypt, Sudan, Saudi Arabia, Yemen, and all of the North African countries from Egypt to and including Morocco. In coming centuries Islam would take over much of Spain and much of the southeastern Mediterranean lands, only to be stopped at the eastern Alps, almost at the walls of Vienna, and also in decisive battles in central France.

During those centuries, many Christian communities in particular lands made their peace with Islam and became respected and protected enclaves within the Muslim world. Just as Jews were often of critical importance to the Islamic rulers—in education, statecraft, economic development, and the like—so also Christians were employed regularly in Muslim enterprises. The great Dome of the Rock in Jerusalem was built by artists and artisans, most of whom were Christians. The intellectual life of Islam benefited greatly from classical Greek and Roman thought, much of it mediated by Christian and Jewish intellectuals. In turn, Muslim thinkers contributed greatly to the preservation and elaboration of the classical and the Jewish and Christian intellectual and spiritual heritages. But all along, Islam viewed the Christian community as having departed from the true faith in the One God, while the Christian community regularly considered Islam as completely hostile to Christian faith, a community of infidels.

Within the Arabic-speaking world, the majority of intellectuals in Christian enclaves held firmly to their classical liturgies and theological understandings, rejecting any serious intellectual or spiritual engagement with Muslim thought. Not even the major Christian effort to retake the Holy Land from Islam changed this situation. In fact, in most regards, the Crusades were a disastrous failure for the Christian world, for this engagement by Christian princes and mercenaries to open up the Middle Eastern trade routes and to gain fortunes for themselves had very little to do with the spread of the Christian gospel among the Islamic-controlled lands.

No doubt, there were many devout Christian believers who joined in the Crusades, or lent their support, for deeply spiritual reasons. The stories of embattled Christian believers in the Holy Land were coming to Europe with increasing frequency as pilgrims made their way to the Middle East. Unhappily, however, the leadership of the forces that moved east under the Christian banners seemed all too ready to plunder and kill as they made their way to the Holy Land, rather than to liberate their Christian brothers and sisters from the yoke of Islam. Rabbi Falk has called attention to the horrors faced by Jewish communities along the Crusaders' path to the Holy Land. Eastern Christians did not fare much better as these Western Christian warriors entered western Asia and the lands of the Middle East. Even so, the Crusaders left their mark on the Holy Land, through the building of churches, the establishment of hospitals, and the planting of religious orders from the West. Following the Crusades, Christianity in the Holy Land would consist of the (dominant) Greek Orthodox Church, with its largely Arabic-speaking membership, smaller numbers of other Orthodox Christians (especially Syrians, Armenians, and Copts), a sizeable number of Greek Catholics, and a sprinkling of others.

In those portions of Spain controlled by Islam from the 700s until their expulsion in the thirteenth century, Islamic, Jewish, and Christian intellectual and spiritual engagements often were quite positive. Islamic culture in Spain reveals the result to this day—in architecture, classical learning, art, and government. Islamic conquerors had often shown greater tolerance for Christian communities than Christian conquerors showed for Muslim communities. When finally the Christian forces succeeded in driving out Islam from Spain, back to western Africa, the Christian state shortly engaged in the persecution of Jews, including their forced conversion to Christianity (often simply simulated by the Jews), and finally expelled them as well (1492), following the lead of Great Britain and France. Islam in southeastern Europe, especially in Albania and in the former Yugoslavia, established enduring communities that were able, with great difficulty, to maintain themselves among their Christian neighbors, both Orthodox and Roman Catholic.

MODERN RELATIONS BETWEEN MUSLIMS AND CHRISTIANS

The growth of Islam after the expulsion of Muslims from Spain and the stabilization of the Islamic population in the Balkans and in western Turkey was largely in Asian and African lands. That growth has been extraordinary in some areas—in the southern Sahara in

Africa, in Indonesia (currently the largest Muslim country, with perhaps as many as 160 million believers), and now in Western Europe and North America, where the Muslim population has increased enormously during the past two decades.

As we have seen, Islam has given a special place to Judaism and Christianity, but that does not mean that there has been a serious, ongoing theological exchange between Muslims and Jews or between Muslims and Christians. Islamic thought has indeed developed into a complex and wide-ranging system of religious belief and practice, but its basic tenets are few and very straightforward, capable of being understood by all believers and followed by those who will. Muslims have felt little need to take with great seriousness the beliefs and practices of the adherents of other religions, not even when the numbers of such adherents were quite large.

The coming of the Industrial Revolution to Muslim lands brought many changes to Turkey, Egypt, Iran, Pakistan, and other Muslim countries. Changes since the Second World War, however, have been enormous. Even as Islam has grown with great rapidity, many Muslim lands have adopted secular approaches to government and international trade, maintaining a structure of Islamic belief in law and custom, in education and culture, but nonetheless becoming for all practical purposes secular states like those in other parts of the world. Even those states like Iran that are determined to maintain their form of Islam as the unifying factor in all aspects of the society are finding it immensely difficult to do so. In Indonesia, such an effort is really unthinkable, given the religious pluralism of that country, with its long Hindu and Buddhist traditions and with a very sizeable Christian population in portions of the country today.

Egypt, which long ago adopted a secular government, is engaged in a major struggle with believers in Islam who consider this move to be a betrayal of Islam. There seems to be little doubt that Islam will have to come to terms with religious pluralism, just as all other religions are being required to do. The fact that Islam has spread in such numbers into Europe and North America, traditionally "Christian" lands, is providing Muslims fresh opportunities to get to know Jewish and Christian neighbors, discuss religion with them, develop ties with the secular, non-Muslim governments of the lands in which they live, and in this way gain the commitment as well as the insight for serious interreligious dialogue and exchange.

CHRISTIAN ARABS AND ISLAM

It is noted above that there are Arabic-speaking Christians who long have lived in Muslim lands, carrying on their faith and traditions as minority groups within the dominant Muslim population, and doing so with great tenacity and fidelity to their ancient Christian heritages. Western Christianity has often ignored these Arabic-speaking Christians, considering them a curiosity. These Christian bodies have a remarkably rich intellectual and spiritual heritage. Syrian Christianity was one of the fastest growing Christian movements in the early centuries. Syrian missionaries took the gospel to eastern Africa and to many parts of Asia, with settlements of Syrian Christians extending as far as the western regions of China. The literature preserved in the Syriac language is massive and complex; only in recent decades have efforts been made to make this body of manuscript literature more readily available to scholars worldwide. Syrian Christians number very few today, but the Syrian heritage is present in many Christian bodies that now depend upon the Latin or Greek or Arabic liturgies.

Coptic Christianity also numbers more than six million in the Middle East, largely in Egypt and the Sudan. These Arabic-speaking Christians still use the ancient Coptic liturgy, but their theologians are actively engaged in ecumenical discussions, including discussions with Muslim neighbors. Coptic Christians often hold positions of leadership within their governments, in professional and business undertakings, and especially in education. Their influence is very great indeed.

Similarly, Ethiopian Christianity, which began to flourish in the ancient kingdom of Aksum in the early fourth century C.E. due to the missionary efforts of Syrian monks, now numbers fifteen million at least, both within Ethiopia and Eritrea and in many countries of Europe and North America, where Ethiopians have settled as a result of conflicts within their homeland. Ethiopian literature is largely Christian literature; it too has been little known until recent years, but specialists in ancient Ethiopic (Ge'ez) are increasing in number, and the literature is receiving remarkably wide attention. Ethiopian Christians also have found it both necessary and possible to confer seriously with their Muslim neighbors as the struggles for new forms of life together among the tribal groupings of Ethiopia have continued. And the massive emigration of Ethiopian Christians throughout the world has placed this great church in closer association with other Christians and also with Islam outside Ethiopia.

The kingdom of Armenia became a Christian nation in the fifth century C.E. Since that time, centuries after the breakup of the nation, Armenian Christians have maintained a distinctive liturgy and Christian theology, have been zealous in preserving their language, culture, and religion in the face of massive pressure and frequent persecution, and are today thriving in many lands. They, too, have a very large Christian literary heritage that is becoming better known as a result of the efforts of believers and scholars in many lands. And they, too, are in an excellent position to engage their Muslim neighbors in intellectual and spiritual exchanges.

Christian literature in the Arabic language is also receiving the attention that it has long deserved. While there has not been an "Arabic" Christianity in the same sense in which there have developed Arabic-speaking Christians with a Greek or Syriac or Coptic or Latin literature and liturgy, the Arabic Christian heritage is nonetheless notable and is being recovered and publicized by a number of scholars in the Middle East and elsewhere. Indeed, Protestant Christianity in the Middle East has contributed a good deal to the study of Arabic Christian literature, especially in connection with efforts to produce a satisfactory Christian Bible in the Arabic language. So also have Roman Catholic efforts devoted to the same end—the production of a literarily and spiritually satisfactory Bible in Arabic. But the study of Arabic-speaking Christianity is being carried on largely by such Arabic-speaking Christians, whether Roman Catholic or Orthodox, whether belonging to one of the ancient churches or recent converts to some branch of Christianity.

We are calling special attention to these Arab Christians because of their importance in deepening the dialogue with Islam. Politically, Arab Christians and their Muslim fellow citizens have joined forces in their struggles for political and social reform—especially in Lebanon, in Egypt, and in the West Bank. Lebanon has long been looked to as one of the major sites for Christian/Muslim dialogue, especially at the American University in Beirut and in other educational institutions where Muslims and Christians study together daily. The American University in Cairo has claimed a similar mission for itself in Egypt. Despite the frightful carnage in Lebanon, the American University and other institutions there still have opportunity to carry forward this undertaking, as do the Egyptian institutions, again despite the rise of militant Islamic groups that have no interest in such undertakings.

The best hope of Arabic Christian and Muslim theological dialogue may lie, however, in the West Bank, as a Palestinian state emerges in which the leadership will surely be both Christian and Muslim. The long struggle of Palestinians for a better life in the occupied territories and in Israel proper has brought Christian and Muslim leaders and thinkers into intimate association, has required fresh efforts for them to understand one another, and may possibly have prepared the soil for deep and serious theological conversation between Christians and Muslims. It is true that at the present time conditions do not encourage this kind of thoughtful spiritual and intellectual exchange. But with the creation of a viable Palestinian state, it should be possible for a new and vital exchange between Muslim and Christian believers to flourish.

In Western Europe and in North America a similar development is taking place. The major advances made by Jews and Christians in interreligious dialogue and study have offered a style of work and a sense of the positive gain to be realized by such efforts. The increasing numbers of Muslims in European and North American universities, studying alongside Christians and Jews, and the increasing number of specialists in Islam who are teaching at these universities have already given considerable impetus to such Muslim/Christian interchanges. Problems remain, of course. Some Muslim scholars who have been critical of certain teachings within Islam have been singled out for attack by Muslim extremists, and some indeed have lost their lives. Non-Muslim specialists in Islam have increased in numbers and are able to deal with Islam with greater freedom, but they, too, often come under attack by extremists, as do Christian specialists who interpret Christianity in ways that fundamentalists object to.

POSSIBILITIES FOR MUSLIM-CHRISTIAN DIALOGUE

Is it realistic at this time of increasing conservatism in both Christianity and Islam to believe that a productive dialogue between Christians and Muslims can take place? The difficulties are surely not to be underestimated. Rabbi Falk has pointed out that there are considerable affinities between Judaism and Islam, affinities not really matched in the relations of Christianity and Islam. Both Judaism and Islam give immense prominence to the divinely revealed law on the basis of which the entire community is to conduct its life. Both give great prominence to the place of classical interpretations of tradition that have augmented the divinely revealed law, a tradition that learned leaders of the community have responsibility to maintain and present to the community. Both stress the relation of religion and state as a positive thing, although both also affirm the rights of minorities within the state.

Christianity lacks these points of connection with Islam. But Christianity has special opportunities as well, even given the hostility of Muhammed to some of the cardinal tenets of Christianity, noted above. One of these is the fact that Arab Christians and Arab Muslims have come to know and respect one another in new and fresh ways during the past five decades in the Middle East. Another promising possibility is the need for a fresh Arabic translation of the Jewish and Christian Bibles, a need long recognized and long worked on, but thus far without real success. What is needed is a major Christian commitment to do its part, with the help of specialists in Islam and in literary Arabic, both Christian and Muslim, to produce a new translation of the Bible into Arabic.

As Kenneth Cragg has pointed out, such an effort could do much to illuminate common themes and theological understandings within the two religions.[3] Instead of studiously avoiding critical theological concepts found in the Koran, the translators should quite self-consciously seek out terms that have commonality within the two traditions. Naturally, it will be necessary not to blur distinctions in the effort to find such points of connection. But as Cragg has gone on to show, such an effort can provide a fresh challenge to both

3. Cragg, *The Arab Christian*, 282-85.

Christian and Muslim theologians to seek to understand their own faith more deeply and fully in the face of the challenge of the other's faith.[4] If the intention is to seek with all one's powers to comprehend the central features of one's own faith as these features offer challenge or problems to the faith of the other, the result is likely to be that those involved will come to understand *both* faiths the better.

Is such an effort really necessary? Many Christian believers may say that it would be a nice thing to do, but that it surely is not essential. Christians may feel no need to relate their faith either to Judaism or to Islam. They may come to see that understanding Judaism is of critical importance, given the history of Christian misunderstanding of Judaism and Christian mistreatment of Jews. But can they be expected to have a similar commitment to enter deeply into the world of Islam, expecting to gain from the effort? Some Christians will of course say yes, since in their judgment Muslims, like all other non-Christians, must be converted to Christianity if they are to receive God's salvation. Other Christians, who surely will want to present Christian faith to Muslims who are ready to listen, will also want to "learn" from the witness and the thought of Islam.

In my judgment, the effort is necessary and urgent. The religion of Islam is a powerful commentary on Christian faith, a challenging and deeply appealing way of understanding life and the world, the character of deity, and the demands of God upon the individual believer and the believing community. Three points of connection offer great promise for the deepening of the Christian's understanding of his or her own faith. The first is reflection on the meaning of the "Oneness" of God. What is at stake in what the Jew and the Muslim so strongly insist upon: that God is One? Have Christians found a satisfactory way to affirm, through the doctrine of the Holy Trinity, that God indeed is One and that at the same time this oneness reflects a oneness in plurality? I believe that a fresh study of God's Oneness, engaged in by Jewish and Christian and Muslim believers and scholars, can deepen the understanding and the faith of all participants. Christian belief in the Trinity rests upon powerful biblical witness in both the Jewish and the Christian Scriptures.

The second point is the place of suffering in the life and thought

4. Ibid., 205-99, with important notes.

of the three religions, human suffering in which the deity—in some way—participates. Islam's great emphasis upon submission is a point of connection. How do the submission of Moses and the prophets to the divine will, the submission of Jesus to the will of the one he called Father, and the submission to Allah that Islam demands relate? Is it perhaps submission in suffering that is the key? If so, can there be a fruitful dialogue between Christians and Muslims on the question of whether Jesus did in fact suffer and die on the cross—a point denied in Muslim teaching? And can Christians not learn much about Islam through the effort to understand why Muhammed insisted that Jesus did not die on the cross?

The third point has to do with the character of the Holy Book, how the divine revelation claims us in connection with the revealed Word. Within the Christian community the question of the Bible's authority is undergoing severe challenge just now; that, however, is only a further reason for a study of the truth, power, beauty, and moral claim of the Holy Book. A three-way engagement among Jews, Christians, and Muslims may be the way to proceed. But one of the ways to make such a study practical would be simply to take up one of the manageable texts of Torah, New Testament, and Koran, texts that address a given subject (though of course in different ways), in order to see concretely how the notion of a revelation through the Word might illuminate the faith and understandings of all parties to the study.

CONCLUSION

Christians and Muslims are living in closer proximity today than they ever have before, and in many more cultural settings than ever before. They have more resources with which to engage in serious debate and dialogue than they have ever had before. Christians in the non-Arabic-speaking world have a wonderful opportunity to turn to Arabic-speaking Christians for help in this undertaking. Christians and Muslims in North America, including especially African American Muslims, have practical reasons for studying the faith of the other, for their children are going to live and work in even greater proximity than they now do, and religious conflicts continue to break out into violence and utter destructiveness.

And perhaps most important of all, Islam is clearly a religion that affirms and builds upon Judaism and Christianity. How can Jews and Christians afford not to take with the greatest possible seriousness the power and truth and beauty and moral strength of this sister religion, even if both Jews and Christians find it necessary to express dissent from some of the tenets and understandings of Islam? My own study of the Koran and of the history and thought of Islam, and my dealings with numbers of Muslim believers, lead me to want to know more. I want the aid of Muslim believers in this quest to understand Islam more precisely. And I want also to speak about the truth and power and beauty and moral strength of Christian faith with my colleague who affirms Islam. As the worldwide population of Muslims approaches that of Christians, I hope that throughout the Muslim and Christian worlds there will arise groups of the two communities who take up the complex task of Muslim/Christian dialogue, using as a helpful guide the ways in which the Jewish and Christian communities have pursued the goal of Jewish/Christian understanding.

SUGGESTED READING

Betts, Robert Brenton. *Christians in the Arab East*. Atlanta: John Knox, 1978.

Cragg, Kenneth. *The Arab Christian*. Louisville: Westminster/John Knox, 1991.

Colbi, Saul P. *A History of the Christian Presence in the Holy Land*. Lanham, Md.: University Press of America, 1988.

Denny, Frederick M., and Rodney L. Taylor, eds. *The Holy Book in Comparative Perspective*. Columbia: University of South Carolina, 1985.

Idinopulos, Thomas A. *Jerusalem Blessed, Jerusalem Cursed: Jews, Christians, and Muslims in the Holy City from David's Time to Our Own*. Chicago: Ivan R. Dee, 1991.

The Koran. Translated with notes by N. J. Dawood. Revised edition. London: Penguin, 1990.

Lippmann, Thomas W. *Understanding Islam: An Introduction to the Muslim World*. Revised edition. New York: Penguin, 1990.

Payne, Robert. *The History of Islam*. Revised edition. New York: Barnes and Noble, 1992.

Schimmel, Annemarie. *Islam: An Introduction*. Albany: State University of New York, 1992.

Trimingham, J. Spencer. *Christianity Among the Arabs in Pre-Islamic Times*. London: Longmans Group, 1979.

CHAPTER SIX

ECONOMIC JUSTICE AND ECOLOGY

A JEWISH OUTLOOK

The Hebrew vocabulary does not include a word that can be translated as "charity." The reason for this is at the very heart of the Jewish concept of economic justice. "The earth is the Lord's, and the fullness thereof" the psalmist sang. With God as the source of all creation, man and woman, God's final act of creation, were destined to serve as stewards of all that preceded them in the orderly pattern of creation. In this role, human beings are committed to share what God has bestowed, and to share their own talents and energies in the building of God's kingdom on earth. This sharing is designated in Hebrew as *tzedakah*, which translates as "justice" or "righteousness." This means that there is no concept of almsgiving in Jewish tradition, but rather a recognition of our responsibility to share equitably God's gifts with all humankind.

Concern for the poor, the widow, and the orphan is the major emphasis in seeking economic justice throughout Hebrew Scriptures. The rabbis taught that "if all afflictions in the world were assembled on one side of the scale and poverty on the other, poverty would outweigh them all" (Midrash, *Exodus Rabbah, Mishpatim* 31:4). The ways in which Jews were to respond to the great needs of the poor are stated quite specifically in the Torah (Pentateuch). It is interesting to note that the concerns are not only for fellow Jews but for the aliens in their midst as well.

First consideration is given to the poor within the community. "If you lend money to my people, to the poor among you, you shall not deal with them as a creditor; you shall not exact interest from them. If you take your neighbor's cloak in pawn, you shall restore it before the sun goes down; for it may be your neighbor's only clothing to use as cover" (Exod. 22:25-27a). Equally important is the equitable sharing of the harvest, enabling the poor to enjoy their own gleanings from God's land: "When you reap the harvest of your land, you shall not reap to the very edges of your field, or gather the gleanings of your harvest. You shall not strip your vineyard bare, or gather the fallen grapes of your vineyard; you shall leave them for the poor and the alien" (Lev. 19:9-10a). The book of Ruth provides a beautiful illustration of how this commandment was followed in biblical times.

The other way in which the land was to be shared with the poor is found in Exodus 23:10-11: "For six years you shall sow your land and gather in its yield; but the seventh year you shall let it rest and lie fallow, so that the poor of your people may eat; and what they leave the wild animals may eat. You shall do the same with your vineyard, and with your olive orchard." All of this is predicated on the recognition that the land belongs to God: "The land shall not be sold in perpetuity, for the land is mine [God's]; with me you are but aliens and tenants. Throughout the land that you hold, you shall provide for the redemption of the land" (Lev. 25:23-24).

Throughout the Torah there are reminders that the laws providing justice for the poor within the Jewish community apply with equal validity to the alien: "You shall not oppress a resident alien; you know the heart of an alien, for you were aliens in the land of Egypt" (Exod. 23:9). This sentiment is echoed in all the books of Torah.

Although it was permitted to enslave the aliens who had been taken captive in war, they were protected from mistreatment and from permanent enslavement by laws such as those found in Exodus 21. However, it was the homeborn who were most zealously protected against enslavement: "If any who are dependent on you become so impoverished that they sell themselves to you, you shall not make them serve as slaves. They shall remain with you as hired or bound laborers. They shall serve with you until the year of the jubilee. Then they and their children with them shall be free from your authority; they shall go back to their own family and to their ancestral property" (Lev. 25:39-41).

The prophets of Israel were deeply concerned that the community adequately follow and enforce those laws that ensured justice for the poor and the oppressed. Jeremiah challenged the wealthy in Judea when he said:

> they have grown fat and sleek.
> They know no limits in deeds of wickedness;
> they do not judge with justice
> the cause of the orphan, to make it prosper,
> and they do not defend the rights of the needy.
> Shall I not punish them for these things?
> says the LORD,
> and shall I not bring retribution
> on a nation such as this?
>
> (Jer. 5:28-29)

The prophet Amos was even more emphatic in his castigation of those responsible for economic injustice in Israel:

> Hear this, you that trample on the needy,
> and bring to ruin the poor of the land,
>
> . . . .
>
> Making the ephah small and the shekel great,
> and practicing deceit with false balances,
> buying the poor for silver
> and the needy for a pair of sandals,
> and selling the sweepings of the wheat. (Amos 8:4, 5b-6)

The teachings of the prophets regarding justice for the impoverished and the underprivileged have been seen throughout the generations as an essential part of the ethical principles of Judaism. The Reform prayerbook for the High Holy Days, *Gates of Repentance*, therefore, includes as one of the scriptural lessons on the morning of Yom Kippur (the Day of Atonement) this mighty challenge from the prophet Isaiah:

> Is such the fast that I choose,
> a day to humble oneself?
> Is it to bow down the head like a bulrush,
> and to lie in sackcloth and ashes?
> Will you call this a fast,
> a day acceptable to the LORD?
>
> Is not this the fast that I choose:
> to loose the bonds of injustice,
> to undo the thongs of the yoke,

> to let the oppressed go free,
>   and to break every yoke?
> Is it not to share your bread with the hungry,
>   and bring the homeless poor into your house;
> when you see the naked, to cover them,
>   and not to hide yourself from your own kin?
>   (Isa. 58:5-7)

All of these teachings are summarized best in two verses from the book of Proverbs. A negative statement is in Proverbs 14:31: "Those who oppress the poor insult their Maker." Put more positively, "Whoever is kind to the poor lends to the LORD" (Prov. 19:17). This theme is continued in the Talmud, where greatest emphasis is placed on helping the poor become self-sufficient: "It is better to lend to a poor person than to give him alms, and best of all is to provide him with capital for business" (Talmud, *Shabbat* 63a). The great medieval philosopher Maimonides echoes this same sentiment in his eight rungs on the ladder of *Tzedakah*. Maimonides taught that the highest rung on the ladder was to prevent a person from becoming poor by providing a loan or a job, so that he can adequately support himself. This is what is meant in Jewish tradition by the term *gemilut chasadim*, an act of lovingkindness, or the real basis for social justice. "No gift is needed by the giving of oneself" (*Mishneh Torah, Hilchot Avadim* 9:8).

Rabbinic writings also translate the ideals of the prophets into the language of the marketplace in terms of duties of employers to employees and workers to their employers, fair prices, the avoidance of false weights and measures, proper business contracts, and fair methods of competition. Richard H. Schwartz relates the teaching of a fourth-century Babylonian rabbi:

> Rav taught the wealthy merchants of his town the importance of scrupulous honesty in business dealings. He stated that on Judgment Day the first question God asks a person is "were you reliable in your business dealings?" (Talmud, *Shabbat*, 31a). The rabbis stress that a person's word is a sacred bond that should not be broken. The Mishnah states that God will exact punishment for those who do not abide by their promises (Baba Metzia 4:2). Cheating a Gentile is considered even worse than cheating a Jew, for "besides being a violation of the moral law, it brings Israel's relig-

ion into contempt, and desecrates the name of Israel's God." (Talmud *Baba Kamma*, 113b)

The sages are very critical of attempts to take away a person's livelihood by unfair competition (Talmud, Sanhedrin 81a). Their overall view of business ethics can be summarized by the verse "better is a little with righteousness than great revenues with injustice." (Proverbs 16:8).[1]

Based on this rich heritage of concern for economic justice as an essential aspect of the ethical principles by which Jews seek to live, the Central Conference of American Rabbis, the rabbinic arm of the Reform movement, has passed a number of resolutions over the years that have addressed specific areas of economic justice. These have included raising the minimum wage established by the federal government, programs for development of low-cost housing and shelters for the homeless, and guarantees for affordable health care for all Americans. In 1994 the Conference passed two resolutions in areas of immediate concern. The first was on Economic Conversion. The background statement for this resolution states in part:

> Jewish tradition affirms again and again that the strength of a society is not in its military and its armaments, but in its people. As it is written, "Not by might and not by power, but by My spirit" (Zechariah 4:6).
>
> The end of the Cold War and the down-sizing of the military are having a serious impact on the economic life of many communities and many individual families. Many communities have become dependent on the production of goods for the military which have little or no application in the consumer economy. Many of those who have worked in these plants and firms have highly specialized skills which likewise have little application in the consumer economy in which many must now find employment.
>
> ... Economic dislocation and unemployment are very painful to communities, families and individuals. Furthermore, the need to change over from military to consumer production is only one factor in communal economic dislocations and increasing unemployment among white collar and technical workers.[2]

1. Richard H. Schwartz, *Judaism and Global Survival* (New York: Atara Publishing Co., 1987) 28-29.
2. CCAR Yearbook, vol. CIV, 118.

The resolutions that followed "urged the Department of Synagogue management to facilitate the creation of job banks at the congregation, regional and national levels" and to "exhort rabbis and local rabbinic organizations to create support groups for the unemployed in our communities, and to become involved in local Economic Conversion projects."[3]

The second C.C.A.R. resolution was "Welfare Reform: From Dependency to Self-sufficiency." The background statement for this resolution stated in part:

> Our tradition teaches that welfare should enhance the dignity of the recipient, have self-sufficiency as its highest form, and enable those unable to attain self-sufficiency to be supported with the basics of life in a manner that keeps the recipient family together.
>
> . . . We believe that the goals of genuine welfare reform can be achieved only through a public/private effort that creates full employment with jobs and wages sufficient to sustain families.
>
> We recognize, however, that until such goals are attained, the nation must continue to relieve the suffering of those in poverty through such programs as Aid to Families with Dependent Children.[4]

The resolutions that followed urged that state and federal legislation to reform the welfare system reflect the following principles: financial self-sufficiency, family stability, and job training and placement. It was also stated that citizenship should not be an eligibility requirement for benefits.

These areas of concern provide a challenge for congregations and national religious organizations to unite across denominational and racial lines to work for the establishment of true economic justice in our cities and our nation.

Closely allied with the Jewish people's deep concern for economic justice is the equally troublesome and critical area of preservation of the environment and fulfilling our role as co-workers with God in conserving and protecting all forms of life in both the natural universe and the animal kingdom. Ultimately ecology has as much to do with the survival of the human race on this earth as does the equitable distribution of goods and services.

3. Ibid., 119.
4. Ibid.

The book of Psalms is filled with magnificent poetry, as in Psalms 8, 24, and 104, that praise God as the Creator of the earth and all that is therein, and that remind human beings that we are God's stewards to protect and maintain God's handiwork. In the Midrash (Ecclesiastes Rabbah 7:28) this responsibility is accompanied by a solemn warning: "In the hour when the Holy One, blessed be He, created the first man, He took him and let him pass before all the trees of the Garden of Eden and said to him: 'See my works, how fine and excellent they are! Now all that I have created, I created for your benefit. Think upon this and do not corrupt and destroy My world, for if you destroy it, there is no one to restore it after you.' "

The Torah is replete with admonitions that men and women must protect the environment. Three examples will have to suffice:

1. *Exodus 23:10-11:* The land must be permitted to lie fallow every seven years (the sabbatical year), so that the poor may eat of its produce and so that the land may rest and renew its fertility.

2. *Deuteronomy 20:19-20:* "If you besiege a town for a long time, making war against it in order to take it, you must not destroy its trees by wielding an ax against them. Although you may take food from them, you must not cut them down. . . . You may destroy only the trees that you know do not produce food."

3. *Deuteronomy 23:13-14:* These verses are an example of the sages' sensitivity to environmental cleanliness. The requirement here is that even in war time care must be taken to dispose of sewage by burying it in the ground, not by dumping it into rivers or littering the countryside.

The rabbis in the Talmud also had much to say about our responsibility for the preservation of the environment and prevention of pollution. They stated that it is forbidden to live in a town that has no garden or greenery (Kiddushin 4:12). Threshing floors had to be placed far enough from a town so that it would not be polluted by chaff carried by winds (Talmud, *Baba Batra* 2:8), and tanneries had to be at least fifty cubits from a town and placed only on the east side of the town, so that odors would not be carried by the prevailing winds from the west (Talmud *Baba Batra* 2:9). Many other similar admonitions are to be found throughout the Talmud.

Jewish tradition has also protected all forms of life, including those whose purpose we may not understand. Maimonides wrote in *The Guide for the Perplexed*: "It should not be believed that all the beings exist for the sake of the existence of humanity. On the contrary, all the other beings too have been intended for their own sakes, and not for the sake of something else." Additionally, the rabbis taught that God created human beings last in order to remind us, lest we grow too proud, that God's entire world precedes us and that we could not have been created had not the rest of it been formed first (Talmud, Sanhedrin 38a).

Our heritage requires that we be cognizant of our obligation to preserve and enhance care and respect for our environment. Many Jewish organizations and Jewish leaders have devoted themselves to eradicating the abuse of our environment and to preserving for future generations those essential properties that enable us to maintain life. At its convention in 1992, the Central Conference of American Rabbis passed two resolutions addressing major problems in conservation of energy and of the environment.

The first resolution dealt with National Energy Strategy. The preamble to the resolution stated, in part: "Our Jewish tradition teaches us that human domain over nature does not include a license to abuse our environment. The Talmudic concept *bal tashchit*, 'do not destroy,' was developed by the rabbis into a universal doctrine that dramatically asserted God's ownership of the land. . . . From this basic concept it follows that any act of destruction is an offense against the property of God. We are destroying our protective ozone layer. We are destroying our oxygen yielding forests. We are destroying our species. We are destroying our future."[5] Therefore the Conference resolved to support the development of a national energy policy centered on conservation and development of alternative energy sources; to oppose offshore drilling, drilling in the Arctic National Wildlife Refuge, and drilling in any environmentally sensitive area; and to call upon federal, state, and local governments to enact legislation that would mandate energy efficiency and develop safe and renewable energy sources.

The second resolution of the C.C.A.R. dealt specifically with the environment. It began with the statement that whereas the environmental crisis for the entire planet has reached the emergency stage, the C.C.A.R. urgently insisted that President George Bush lead the

5. Ibid., vol. CII, 193-94.

United States delegation to the U.N. Conference on Environment and Development in Brazil, and that the United States delegation attend the UNCED without preconceived limitations on the actions to be taken in concert with other nations of the planet—and go with open minds and serious concern for the survival of humanity, which is imminently threatened.[6]

Other vital environmental concerns with which the Social Action Commission of the Union of American Hebrew Congregations has been involved, in concert with many Christian groups in Washington, D.C., are the exploding populations of the world and their relationship to global warming and the Ecojustice Movement, which recognizes that environmental problems affect primarily the poor and minorities in the United States and in Third World nations.

The importance of religious leadership in protecting our environment is highlighted by an article by Ronald J. Sider, Professor of Theology and Culture at Eastern Baptist Theological Seminary. The article, which appeared in the spring 1995 issue of *The Amicus Journal*, a publication of the Natural Resources Defense Council, informs us that "in 1990, a group of renowned scientists signed an 'Open Letter to the Religious Community,' urging religious people to join the movement to save the environment. In their statement, the scientists acknowledged that the ecological threat is so great that we cannot avoid disaster unless the religious community joins the struggle."

Sider encourages us "that this is beginning to happen in important ways. On Earth Day 1994, Christians and Jews in the United States mailed out environmental kits to 53,800 congregations all across the country. A follow-up kit is being mailed out this year [1995]. This effort and a wide range of related activities are the work of the National Religious Partnership for the Environment. The Partnership is a coalition of four groups: the U.S. Catholic Conference, the National Council of Churches, the Evangelical Environmental Network, and the Coalition on Jewish Life and the Environment."

Our biblical heritage provides a firm foundation for interfaith activity that will undergird efforts to protect and preserve our environment. The call for religionists and scientists to join hands in providing leadership in seeking worldwide cooperation to save our

6. Ibid., 194.

planet deserves our best effort to fulfill our role of stewards of God's creation.

SUGGESTED READING

Gower, Joseph F., ed. *Religion and Economic Ethics*. Lanham, Md.: University Press of America, 1960.

"Justice," *Encyclopedia Judaica*, vol. 10. Jerusalem: Keter Publishing House, 1971.

Neusner, Jacob. *The Economics of the Mishnah*. Chicago: The University of Chicago Press, 1990.

Patterson, David, and Lily Edelman, eds. *Judaism and Human Rights*. New York: W. W. Norton & Co., 1972.

Schwartz, Richard H. *Judaism and Global Survival*. New York: Atara Publishing Co., 1987.

Stringfellow, William. *Dissenter in a Great Society*. Nashville: Abingdon Press, 1966.

Vorspan, Albert, and David Saperstein. *Tough Choices: Jewish Perspectives on Social Justice*. New York: UAHC Press, 1992.

ECONOMIC JUSTICE AND ECOLOGY

A CHRISTIAN OUTLOOK

According to Scripture, God demands that the human community care for the creation as God's good gift of love, intended for all living beings. Indeed, the very mountains and streams and the soil and the winds, the seas and the stars and planets—inanimate by most definitions—also are created by God and cared for by God. But the Bible places enormous responsibility on the human community to care for the whole of creation, under God's direction. Psalm 8 is one of the great texts in support of this understanding. Human beings may be small and frail in relation to other creatures, but it is precisely the human community that is placed in charge of the *whole* of God's creation—sheep, oxen, beasts of the field, birds of the air, fish of the sea, and even the great sea monster who "passes along the paths of the sea" (Ps. 8:8). This fact ties together the Bible's demand for economic justice and for a wise and generous commitment to care for the totality of the earth—its air, its ozone layer, its seas, its streams, its soil, its plant and animal life, and its human dwellers.

The two concerns belong together because both involve responsible dealings with God's gifts of creation. God did not create some human beings for the purpose of their owning so much of the goods of earth that others would necessarily have too little. Disparities in wealth and control of earth's goods do exist, of course, and no doubt will exist. But it was not a part of God's purpose in creation that some lands should control enormous wealth and others suffer as a consequence. The Bible does not teach that God purposes an equal sharing of earth's goods; it does insist that there be a fair sharing of the divine gifts.

148

Similarly, God did not indicate that a certain generation of human beings should enjoy the goods of earth at the expense of later generations. The command in Genesis 1 is to "be fruitful, multiply, fill the earth, and subdue it." The earth is capable, with human help, of going beyond the fertility and support of life that it would offer naturally, or that it provides at any given time. The Bible insists that nature is not divine; no doubt, there is a marvelous balance of nature, but that balance, that givenness, is only enhanced when human beings fulfill the destiny that God purposed for them. It is, of course, true that, in many respects, human civilization has damaged and corrupted and despoiled God's creation. But human civilization has also enhanced and transformed the divine creation, making it possible for billions more human beings to find a home on our planet, without the necessity for the annihilation of the non-human parts of the creation. The Bible is not sentimental about the natural world. It insists that human beings, under God's guidance and with the aid of the gifts God has entrusted to human beings, are to enhance the Creator's work, to bring it toward its intended purpose. If that is to happen, a tolerable system of justice must prevail on earth, among all peoples, and no given generation of human beings must act as if it were the last generation to inhabit the planet.

The Bible, however, puts these concerns squarely upon the heart and mind of the covenant people—Israel and the community of the New Covenant. The Jewish and Christian communities are charged to affirm and explain, to uphold and insist upon both economic and social justice and care for the health and future of the planet. As Rabbi Falk has shown, the prophets of Israel were unrelenting in their demand for social justice on the part of all the peoples of earth, but especially on the part of God's people Israel. The same applies to the teachings of Jesus, as we have noted in earlier discussions. Jesus demands just the quality of life on earth that God purposes for all peoples, but Jesus insists upon it within the community of those who recognize, with him, the nearness of the rule of God. In the light of what God is bringing to earth here and now, the community of Christian believers is charged urgently to see to earth's needs and to labor for a community of believers that is "salt" for the earth, and a light for the world.

THE CONTEMPORARY SITUATION

When we look at our world we may be tempted to doubt that Jews and Christians, despite their beliefs and their heritage, can do anything to help realize these noble ideals and commitments. Rich nations get richer at the expense of the poorer nations. And often the poorer nations are plundered by their own citizens, creating even greater poverty and social dislocation. The very means that bring wealth to some often despoil the creation, leaving huge problems for the next generations, generations that are also intended to share in God's good gifts. The command to human beings to care for God's earth seems to have been taken up as a warrant to claim it all for one generation or for particular nations or for particular individuals.

It would be shortsighted, however, to view the contemporary situation only in this way. The very advances in technology and knowledge of the planet that have given some nations and groups great wealth and have tempted them to exploit the earth or other nations and peoples are advances that offer the prospect of a greater level of economic justice and a more manageable stewardship of the earth for the sake of generations to come, and for earth's own sake. The technological revolutions of our own day bring the means for the spread of economic and social justice, even as they are accompanied by the spread of greed and social destruction. And therein lies the hope and promise that the biblical vision of economic justice and of a blessed and healthy planet can find increasing realization in our day.

CHRISTIAN EFFORTS TO REALIZE ECONOMIC JUSTICE

Early Christianity accepted the Hebrew Scriptures as its own Scriptures, thereby claiming as its own both the promises and the demands of the revelation of God to Israel. New features did appear, as we have noted above. For a time after the resurrection of Jesus, the Christian community, which grew rapidly after Pentecost Day (see Acts 2), shared all goods and needs in common, but that experiment was not to last for long. During the time when the church was a small and struggling new religious force in the Roman Empire, questions of economic justice and ecology were largely local issues within the various communities where Christians lived. But with the spread of Christianity within the Hellenistic world, new problems arose, for now the Christians were living no longer as a form of Judaism but had broken with Judaism to become a separate and distinct religious community. The customs and laws of Hellenistic and Roman society often clashed with those of the Jewish community within which Christianity had arisen. The apostle Paul struggled with this question, as we can see from his letters to churches in Galatia, in Corinth, and in Rome. But the message of the Torah, God's Law, remained, even as some of its ceremonial and dietary customs and requirements were laid aside. So did the prophetic call for public justice, for fair dealings in business, for fair treatment of the poor and helping them to become self-sufficient.

Caring for the needs of fellow Christians loomed large. It was intolerable for Paul to see the Christian community failing to meet the needs of its own members, going to public officials to settle claims against a member of the community (see 1 Corinthians 6), and the like. Paul's great effort to collect funds for the struggling Jerusalem Church shows how important this concern for the whole Christian body was, for it was an affirmation of the church's unity; the Christian community was one worldwide fellowship of believers, bound to one another by the divine love with which they had been brought into the fellowship. But the more urgent criterion was the simple fact of human need; when persons were hungry or ill-clothed or ill-housed or without family or friends or suffering bodily or other pain they were the special concern for the risen Christ, and thus they were the special concern of the church. The picture of the Son of Man coming in glory to render judgment upon all the earth (Matt. 25:31-46) makes this clear. Where in particular is the risen Christ to be found in our world? Among the poor and the suffering and the lonely and the despised of earth. Ministering to the needy thus becomes, for the Christian community, not only a service to be rendered but also a way of sharing life with the risen Christ.

When Christianity became the official religion of the Roman Empire, massive changes occurred. Now it was in the interest of the churches of particular lands and of the empire for the state to prosper and for those in positions of authority to look with favor upon the church and its officials. As we noted above, bishops of the church served as magistrates, handling many civic concerns. The church thus had to develop a system of laws and understandings on the basis of which it could do its part in maintaining justice within the state. Tempted often to favor its own interests rather than those of public justice, and tempted often to ignore the needs of the poor and the mistreated, the church nevertheless found ways to fulfill this responsibility. In the course of doing so the church took the lead in developing what has been called a Christian civilization, a society in which the commitments and understandings of the Jewish and Christian heritages gave tone and character, and often explicit direction, to the state.

By medieval times, especially in the work of Thomas Aquinas, a whole body of theory and teaching on economic and social justice had developed, building upon Scripture but also borrowing strongly from Greek and Roman understandings and practices. In the Roman Catholic community this theology of economic and social justice continues to be of enormous value. It was greatly expanded in the late nineteenth and twentieth centuries on the basis of newer views of government and society, and it has now become a valuable part of the Christian teaching on economic justice for all Christians.

The labor movement owes much to this Christian theory of economic justice that affirms, in public and politically usable form, the central message of Israel's prophets and of Jesus. While the notion of "Christian" states has had to change markedly, the efforts through the centuries to take the lead in ministry to the needy, in calling to account those who preyed upon others and made themselves wealthy by robbing others and despoiling the earth, and in developing workable systems and means of assuring tolerable justice for all—all are a part of the glory of Christian history.

This glory is evident especially in the development of institutions to care for the sick and the needy and the orphaned, and to provide education for the community. Most hospitals, orphanages, agencies for the elderly and for youth, and especially the academies, colleges, and universities arose at the initiative of the church and the Jewish community. The church also contributed massively to the elimination of slavery, even though Christian apologists for the institution sought to show that this barbarous practice was acceptable. And the introduction of child labor laws throughout the industrialized world came about largely through the pressures of visionary Christian and Jewish individuals and with the backing of much church leadership—again, despite the fact that the reform was too slow in coming and was resisted by other church voices.

During the last one hundred years in the United States, the church has been the prime mover in a number of major social reform efforts. For example, in the Social Gospel movement of the late nineteenth and early twentieth centuries, Christian leaders like Walter Rauschenbusch reaffirmed and made credible for many Christians that human beings had the capacity, under God, to work a real revolution in human affairs, providing for the needs of all, securing liberty and a sense of worth and purpose for all, and in the process bringing warfare among nations to an end. While some leaders of the Social Gospel movement (not Rauschenbusch, however!) may have believed too strongly in human progress, underestimating the depth of human temptation to evil and destruction, this confidence in the possibilities open to the human community to ease human suffering and move toward a wholesome and just community worldwide is badly needed today.

Another of the great gains, noted in chapter 3, is in the field of racial justice, although there too—as we noted—the injustices persist, made evident especially by the increasing economic gap between whites and African Americans. The economic gains within the African American community are remarkable, even though young black men remain the most vulnerable group within American society.

Similarly, women have made great economic gains within the society, often under the leadership of courageous and farseeing Christian women and some men, once again despite the fact that the church has been slow to insist that women and men have equal responsibility for the church's ministry. The salary disparity between women and men in church vocations shows that equal justice is still to be achieved.

Many challenges face church and synagogue today, as Rabbi Falk has pointed out. Both communities need to be careful not to lose heart as the political tide seems to move against "big government" and toward freedom from any kind of constraint on the lives of individuals, associations, and businesses. Both Jewish and Christian faiths warn against placing too great confidence in the purity of the human heart and will. Individuals need the help of neighbors to fulfill their responsibilities, and Christians need the help of fellow Christians to live the Christian life. Who can deny that while Jewish and Christian folk have taken the lead in many of the reforms of the past decades, it has been action by the legislatures, the courts, and the executive offices that brought those commitments into force within the society. The church needs to call its members to active political action in behalf of a wholesome and fair economic system, with necessary governmental restraints to stem greed and the temptation to exploit.

One of the remarkable gains of the past three decades has been the emergence of a fresh commitment to care for this blesssed earth that supports all of life. The church has done a fair job of bringing the resources of Jewish and Christian faith to bear upon ecological issues. One feature that needs greater stress is God's creation of a richly complex and varied world in which all the parts depend upon one another and draw life and strength from one another. There are not great numbers of biblical texts that affirm this "balance" of nature, of course; the notion was not a conscious one in earlier times. But Psalm 104, drawing inspiration from an ancient Egyptian poem in praise of the Aten, the sun deity, does affirm this interdependence, this beauty, and it also stresses God's love and care for inanimate and nonhuman parts of the creation. Note in this psalm how rivers and streams flow down from the mountains that God has raised up, giving nurture to plants and grass and animals and human beings. Trees grow beside the stream, offering a nesting place for storks, and storks are created to nest in the trees. Wild mountain fastnesses are created for rock badgers, and the badgers are created for the rocky terrain. Steep mountain ridges are formed to provide a habitat for the wild mountain goats, and the mountain goats are created for the mountains. Even the vast seas contain the great sea monster, formed by God to sport in it. There is here a marvelous picture of the natural world that has in it a place for human beings that is not exalted above that of the other creations of God.

But all of it depends, at every moment, upon the divine breath or spirit to give it its continued life and being. Should God for an instant withdraw that breath, all living things would cease to have life and would return to dust. At the same time, the psalm shows no thought that God is about to do so. The psalm sees only one really discordant note in the whole of creation—sinners! Sinners are those who break the bounds, who do not care for their part of the creation, who do not live in harmony with their counterpart creatures. What a marvelous text in support of the ecological revolution that has brought renewed health to the planet—to its air and seas and soil and vegetation and fauna.

HOPEFUL SIGNS IN THE STRUGGLE FOR A JUST AND SAFE WORLD

Are there signs of hope that the Christian community worldwide is contributing in fresh ways to the struggle for a just world and for a physical and cultural environment that is supportive of God's revealed purposes? I am confident that there are. The first is the sheer fact of religious pluralism and diversity in a world in which all lands, peoples, and cultures know a good deal about the others. Economic injustice is a universally known fact; no country and no people is ignorant of the fact, or the extent, of economic disparities between the "haves" and the "have nots." The Christian community has helped to make known this widespread injustice, and the result has been that some lands have undergone remarkable transformation. South Africa, for example, is a massively wealthy nation. Its economic opportunities are now being opened up for many more of its citizens. Namibia is a democratic nation in which the same thing is happening. The new Vietnam may be on the brink of a new and freer economic society that will benefit many more of its citizens, perhaps paving the way for many of its former citizens to return to their homeland. And despite the dislocations in the former Soviet Union, numbers of the new states may find fresh opportunity for the sharing of earth's goods on a more equitable basis. And many Latin American lands are enjoying new freedoms and prosperity. And all of this is occurring at the very time that fresh dangers lurk on the horizon and many millions of individuals worldwide are continuing to suffer deprivation and oppression. There is clearly no reason for complacency, but there is reason to affirm the positive developments that often get little attention in the worldwide press.

A second reason for hope is the sheer fact that all the nations and peoples of earth today know of dangers to the environment, recognize the cost of pollution of our planet and the destruction of its flora and fauna. Much has already been done to slow down the pollution; some streams and lakes are again clear, and many communities are organized to further ecological concerns. Even as the struggles continue to save some part of the Amazon rain forest, for example, new groups of Christian people are becoming much more active and much more sophisticated in presenting their case.

What is lacking is a much more effective infrastructure than we currently have within the Christian world. Each church body provides its own programs, locally, regionally, nationally, and worldwide, it seems. The Councils of Churches do what they can, but so many Christians have lost their once-strong commitment to ecumenism that the Councils work with entirely too little support. Ways must be found for the world Christian community to agree on simple, uncomplicated agendas for the increase of economic and social justice on the planet. A similar agenda must develop for the Christian community on ecological questions.

Of course, the Christian community is sharply divided on questions of economic justice and ecology, just as it is on virtually all of the issues discussed in earlier chapters. The agenda developed, therefore, must be basic. It must concentrate not so much on what the nations of earth *must do,* but on what they *simply must not do, must not let happen.* The church is in its strongest position when it, like the prophets, declares what is simply not in the will and purpose of God and calls the nations to help stop actions that are destroying human life and destroying our planet. The agenda should begin with a cry like that of the widow in the parable of the unjust judge (Luke 18). The widow does not tell the judge exactly how to adjudicate her case; she simply demands justice, vindication. She will not let the judge have peace until he takes her case in hand and renders judgment. The church and the synagogue have one massive resource that is entirely too little used: their voice of protest. Think of the terrible and powerful line in Isaiah 64:1: "O that you [God] would tear open the heavens and come down!" The community prays that God will come and see just how terrible things are; we need also to let the political leaders of our land and all lands hear our cry for justice, for relief.

Once that outcry is really raised, those who cry out will surely find one another and begin to shape a more effective strategy for securing a more just and safer world—locally, regionally, nationally, and internationally.

Another area of hope is the church's newfound skill in using its property and wealth to help build a better community. Many African American congregations have found that they can purchase land around the church building, renovate it, provide better housing for the community, help start new and needed businesses, develop services for children and the elderly and for young mothers, and enhance the life of faith while helping create a safer and more economically sound living environment. Given the extraordinary wealth of Christian congregations worldwide, the time is ripe for many thousands of congregations to do what these African American congregations are doing. Church property, much of it, still lies unused during much of the week. Some of it, no doubt, should be sold and the proceeds used wisely, for we know that many communities have entirely too many church buildings to keep in repair. But thousands of others need to become centers of work for justice and for an environmentally safe world. Partnerships between congregations and secular service organizations are increasing, and they need to increase even more.

Another great source of hope is the ecumenical church itself. In many parts of Asia and Latin America new forms of church life have emerged that are helping to transform the social order. Even among very conservative evangelical communities in many lands, where the struggle for public justice has not been a high priority in the past, this commitment to transform the social order is unmistakable. The commitment to economic justice is powerful in African and Latin American Christian communities, and new agendas are even now being forged in these lands.

LOCAL, SYMBOLIC ACTS

We often underestimate the value of specific acts in behalf of justice by local groups. Not every congregation can work equally well on all aspects of a social justice agenda. The important thing is to *begin*. Within a single congregation, one task force can galvanize the life and work of the entire local community. On all the issues discussed in previous chapters the same is true. When an individual or a community acts in behalf of some particular cause, it is committing itself to a way of life in the world that includes the other planks in a social action agenda. Not everything can be done at once, and no congregation can confront the entire justice agenda. But when we act on a particular cause, we identify ourselves publicly as being among those who will not let injustice in the world go unchallenged, who will not let the earth be made uninhabitable for a next generation.

We should note how interrelated are the causes of racial justice, economic justice, war and peace, ecology, and the other topics reviewed above. For example, if the planet is to be able to support a world population adequately, that population ought not simply to grow without restraint. On the other hand, this current generation ought not to suppose that its size is the optimal size for the planet's health. Here, too, God's mandate to the human community to care for the earth reaches out into all features and facets of individual, social, and political life. Population control is surely necessary, but there is room for debate as to the optimal population that the planet can sustain—both human and nonhuman.

In our closing chapter we will discuss the place of vision and ultimate hope in God as an incentive for Jewish and Christian ethics and for moral behavior on the part of individuals, groups, and national and international communities.

SUGGESTED READING

Braybrooke, Marcus. *Stepping Stones to a Global Ethic*. London: SCM Press, 1992.

Gore, Al. *Earth in the Balance: Ecology and the Human Spirit*. New York: Penguin Books, 1992.

Gutiérrez, Gustavo. *A Theology of Liberation*. Revised Edition. Maryknoll, N.Y.: Orbis Books, 1988.

Haan, Roelf L. *The Economics of Honour: Biblical Reflections on Money and Property*. Geneva: WCC Publications, 1996.

Kung, Hans. *Global Responsibility: In Search of a New World Ethic*. New York: Crossroads Publishing Co., 1991.

McDaniel, Jay B. *Earth, Sky, Gods & Mortals: Developing an Ecological Spirituality*. Mystic, Conn.: Twenty-Third Publications, 1990.

Religion and Economic Justice. Philadelphia: Temple University Press, 1991.

A CHRISTIAN OUTLOOK

Rethinking Materialism: Perspectives on the Spiritual Dimension of Economic Behavior.
Grand Rapids, Mich.: Eerdmans, 1995.
Romero, Archbishop Oscar. *Voice of the Voiceless: The Four Pastoral Letters and Other Statements.* Maryknoll, N.Y.: Orbis Books, 1985.

CHAPTER SEVEN

JEWISH AND CHRISTIAN ETHICS IN THE LIGHT OF GOD'S PROMISES

INTRODUCTION

Human beings act on the basis of many motives and many combinations of motives. We act on the basis of custom, habit, those elements of our upbringing in a given culture that become the norms of our behavior, just as they are the norms of the behavior of our group and our community. It is good that much of human moral activity is of this sort, for ingrained custom is the cement that holds a society together. Sadly in our day, many individuals grow up with a terribly deficient sense of what it means to be a person, how human beings behave, what the guidelines and norms for our community are. The disintegration of values that is often spoken of today rests very largely in this fact: Entirely too many of our fellow citizens lack that sense of customary morality that is central to the moral life. It is notoriously difficult to provide such a foundational sense of right and wrong in later years, once childhood has passed.

For most of us, however, even in our permissive and loose society, tradition is still immensely important. It is what comes to us through Scripture, through family, through synagogue and church, and through local community. But there are other important motives for human behavior. One of these is the desire to please God. Fear of God's displeasure constitutes much of the religious motivation for the moral life. The psalmist said: "The fear of the LORD is the beginning of wisdom." This is entirely appropriate, so long as fear is not the only motivation.

Jewish tradition is pervaded by a basic confidence in our human ability to do the right thing. Judaism contains relatively little of the pessimism or fatalism about the human condition that one senses in other theologies. Hebrew Scriptures (for example, Gen. 6:5 and 8:21) preserve a remarkable appreciation of our ability to do both good and evil. Every moment of our lives can bring us into complex relationships where values are in conflict, and where it may not be clear as to how we should act. The Jew is expected to confront each situation with the question: What is it that God demands of me? The answer is the mitzvah.

Mitzvah is from the Hebrew verb meaning "to command." A mitzvah, therefore, is a commandment (from God). To fulfill the 613 commandments in the written and the oral law is to do what is good in God's sight. Therefore, a mitzvah is a good deed, in response to God's commandments. To be a member of the Jewish community, therefore, is to bind ourselves to be partners with God, ushering in God's kingdom of righteousness on earth through obedience to the moral Law.

Another highly important motive for the moral life is simply our reasoned view of the aptness, the rightness, the pleasingness of a particular mode of behavior. The philosopher Immanuel Kant generalized this motive, which he thought the best of all motives, into a version of the Golden Rule: "Do unto others as you would have others do unto you." Kant's way of putting the maxim is, "Act in such a way that you would be pleased to have your mode of action become the universal mode of action." That is, I should act in such fashion as to desire that everyone else would act, toward me and all others, in the same way. This is a noble and powerful motive for the moral life. One could say that rational beings should always follow a universal moral norm. And even if a whole community cannot agree on what that universal norm is, individuals and groups within the community can follow Kant in saying that they commit themselves to follow the very norm of conduct to which they would like all others to conform.

Another powerful motive for human moral activity is to do what we believe our Master, our Teacher, our God would have us do—not only on the basis of revealed Law, but also quite simply because we are convinced that this is what the Master would have us do. For Christians, "What would Jesus do?" has been the norm and motive

161

for much moral action through the centuries. Jesus was a peacemaker; we also will be peacemakers. Jesus was a friend of sinners; we, too, will be friends of sinners. Jesus worked acts of healing; we also will become healers, to the fullest extent of our abilities. "Follow me!" is a command from our Lord that is of immense power for the moral life, for we want to be like Jesus.

One other motivation needs to be underscored: a motivation that derives from the disclosures of what God is bringing about in the world, what God's own goals and objectives for the planet are understood to be. The prophets of Israel offered marvelous pictures of the coming day on which God's purposes for Israel and for all the creation would find realization. These pictures of God's "kingdom," as Jesus spoke of the day, rest, of course, upon the experience and longing of the human heart. Some of these visions even depict the transformation of the creation beyond the human community into nothing less than a "new heaven and a new earth," even though none of them actually suggests a "return" to some original paradise. Prophetic visions always point forward, portraying something new, even though modeled on what the human mind and heart long for today.

The Hebrew prophets and Jesus make it entirely clear that this coming day of the fulfilling of God's purposes affects every member of the covenant community in a special way. If that is the kind of world that God is bringing, then God wants us to join in the bringing of that world. The prophetic visions and Jesus' portrayal of the kingdom of God are invitations to the believing community to join God in the realization of the vision. The community committed to God's cause is to live now, in company with God and with God's help, as a community committed to the kind of world that God is bringing to birth.

GOD'S PROMISES TO ISRAEL

What are these promises of God to Israel on the strength of which the people of Israel are motivated to live their lives, joining God in the realization of the promises made? The covenants are good affirmations of the promises. Noah (Genesis 8–9) and all humankind are promised a safe world, never again to be threatened with destruction by universal flood (or other such catastrophes that utterly destroy the divine creation). Abraham (Genesis 12) is promised that God will be with him, that Abraham will have many descendants, a land as God's gift, and that, through Abraham, God's blessings will extend to "all the families of earth."

Moses has the promise of God to Abraham reaffirmed for Moses and for the people of Israel. To the earlier promise, God provides the gift of the Law, and God promises to accompany Moses, offering protection and guidance, as Moses leads the people into the land promised by God. This promise is reaffirmed to David, God's chosen leader of Israel, and in addition, David is promised that God will see to it that a descendant of David will continue always to be present to offer leadership for the people of God.

Israel's prophets, however, give us the fullest and most varied portrayals of what it will be like when God's promised rule on earth actually comes to pass. There are five dominant images in these varied pictures of the fulfillment of God's promises. The first takes up the earlier promise made to David and his household, speaking of a new ruler who will govern the people of God justly and whose rule will mean blessing for the nations of earth as well. While there are many pictures of this promised ruler, the ones that give us the clearest clues to its power and meaning are found in Isaiah 9 and 11, Micah 5, and Zechariah 9. In those texts, the prophets speak of a ruler, clearly patterned after the figure of David, a "man after God's own heart," who does not rule as ordinary rulers ruled—not even David—but who rules in righteousness, whose commitment is to peace with justice, and whose governing means good news, not bad, for all other nations and peoples of earth. Over and over again the emphasis falls upon the peace that this ruler, under God's guidance and in God's power, brings to earth. "Prince of Peace" is an apt designation of this ruler.

A second image, prominent especially in texts from the book of Isaiah (chapters 2; 35; 40) and in the Psalms (24; 27; 46; 48; 76; and many more), portrays the city of Jerusalem as God purposes it to be: the haven of the oppressed, the joy of the whole earth, earth's very center, secure and yielding blessing for all peoples and nations. The emphasis falls not so much upon Jerusalem as the center of sacrifices, although of course that is surely important. Rather, the emphasis in most of these texts is laid upon what Zion, the other name for Jerusalem, does to bring God's own presence to earth—glorious, palpable, unmistakable. Emphases may fall upon the restoration of the Temple, its personnel, and the strict observance of the divine will, as in Ezekiel. But even then, what the Temple does is to give life, healing, hope, and delight in God's presence.

A third image from the prophets stresses changes in the very character and makeup of God's people Israel. Jeremiah speaks of a new covenant (chapter 31), while Ezekiel speaks of a new heart and a new spirit (chapter 36). Here, the relationship with God is a cleansing, a wrenching, a transformation of the very being of the people of God. But the emphasis does not fall upon judgment and then restoration; the judgment is understood to have befallen Israel already. Israel's Babylonian captivity clearly prompts the framing of this image, as prophets reflect on the question, "Has God utterly rejected the people of God?" The answer is a resounding no. Even so, Israel is not simply restored to some former condition or situation; Israel is transformed. New heart, new spirit, new covenant— these are the dominant terms.

A fourth image speaks in more sweeping terms of a transformed people living on a transformed land. Here, the weight of emphasis falls upon God's reaffirming the promise of exodus and re-entry into the land of promise and on the effects of this divine action on earth itself. Wilderness and dry land blossom and flourish; the trees of the forest clap their hands. Waters gush out from beneath the hill of Zion to water the earth, turning the Dead Sea into a fresh-water lake. Animals live harmoniously with human beings, and no one hurts or seeks to destroy another. These images abound in the prophetic literature, including some of the texts already mentioned (Isaiah 11 and 35, for example). One text, which may be the most sweeping of all, speaks of God's providing a highway back to Zion and to the land of promise, a highway on which all those wounded and despised and neglected of earth find the fulfillment of their lives. This text is Isaiah 35, where verse 8 may be translated:

> A highway shall be there, a way;
> it shall be called the Holy Way.
> The unclean shall not pass it by;
> it shall be for them (as well).

No travelers, not even the simple ones,
shall lose their way.[1]

The prophet Ezekiel (especially in chapters 40–48) speaks of a transformed land of Israel, equally divided among the tribes, with provision made for the blessings of temple worship to fall equally upon all. Zechariah speaks of a Zion that expands to such an extent that no one can know except God alone who will be among its new citizens (Zechariah 2; see also 4 Ezra 9–10). In these and many other texts, the second image regarding Zion and the third image depicting a transformed people are artfully woven together to provide an almost cosmic picture of the consummation of God's work.

Late in the prophetic tradition there comes an even more comprehensive picture of the fulfillment of God's work on earth: the vision of a "new heaven and a new earth." In most of its occurrences (as in Isaiah 24–27 and Ezekiel 38–39) the picture is still clearly tied to the present historical realm. While often there is a display of divine wrath and judgment that may threaten both the natural and the historical world, God's acts of restoration and re-creation are firmly connected to the present creation. Only in later, postbiblical texts (for example, 4 Ezra 11-12 and 13) do we have pictures of God's starting over, bringing utter ruin to the first creation as the second supplants it. And even in those later apocalyptic texts, the writers do envisage continuity between the two ages, for God does preserve a faithful remnant.

The most beautiful and powerful of the occurrences of this fifth image comes in Isaiah 65:17–66:24. This text, though marred by an occasional spirit of bitterness and vindictiveness against God's enemies (see 66:22-24), presents God as the restorer of Zion and its people, tenderly caring for them, providing utter security and safety, blessing and richness of life, for the people of God. This transformation of Zion clearly involves the transformation of the conditions of life on earth: The lifespan of human beings is greatly extended, the sense of joy and delight in life is deepened, and apparently (though this is not explicitly said) Zion's new glorification has positive consequences for the entire earth. The text repeats from Isaiah 11 the promise of harmony and peace among animals as well as among the nations.

1. Translation by Walter Harrelson. See the footnotes to Isa. 35:8 in the NRSV.

These, then, are the five dominant images of consummation of God's purposes for the creation. Sometimes the emphasis falls upon the leader of Israel, God's chosen agent in bringing consummation. More often, the emphasis lies on Zion, earth's center, the site of the worship and praise of God and the site of God's own loving concern for all the creatures of God, especially for those beloved faithful who render God praise. Sometimes the weight of emphasis falls upon needed moral and spiritual changes within the human community, and occasionally the entire natural world is included in those changes. And late in the prophetic period, speculation about whether this sinful earth is actually redeemable at all begins to appear. Apocalyptic visions of God's sweeping away one world in order to create a new world begin to emerge. But the prophetic heritage, and Judaism throughout the continuing centuries, has resisted this position. No matter how dire the times may be, God does not destroy one world to make way for another. The goodness of God's creation stands, and the promise of God to Noah stands.

PROMISES TO THE CHURCH

This set of images was clearly dominant in the message of John the Baptist and in Jesus' message. According to the Gospels, John begins with a call to Israel to prepare the way of the Lord, using the language of Isaiah 40. His message is a call to repentance, with stern warnings to those who do not heed the call. Jesus, too, calls for repentance, but his basic summons is the announcement of the nearness of what Israel's prophets had promised. The time for God's transformation of life on earth is at hand, and the people of the Covenant are those to whom Jesus addresses the announcement of that time.

In the Gospels, the various elements of the prophetic promises outlined above seem to have merged, in Jesus' parables and teachings, into one dominant image: the rule of God, a rule that God is bringing to earth here and now. Scholars are still divided over the question of whether, and if so when, Jesus identified himself as the bringer, on God's behalf, of the rule of God. Was he announcing a "coming" Son of Man (using the language of Daniel 7) who would usher in God's rule? Was he making such an announcement and leaving open the question of whether God had a special vocation for him in the coming consummation? Or was he, from early in his ministry, confident of the centrality of his own place in the bringing of the divine rule? The available evidence does not settle this question; it is an issue that resolves itself in the life of the believing community. There, Christians come to identify the rule of God with the person and the work of Jesus the Christ.

We should remember, however, that the import of the "rule of God" or "kingdom of God" imagery surely was made the clearer by Jesus' acceptance of the imagery of Israel's prophets. The first recorded address or sermon of Jesus in a synagogue is reported in Luke 4. The text Jesus used was Isaiah 61, one of the texts that speak of a coming ruler who will bring to consummation God's work on earth. And according to Luke, Jesus affirms, "Today this scripture has been fulfilled in your hearing."

Other New Testament images seem to touch upon the fifth image mentioned above: the New Heaven and New Earth. Paul seems to have been caught up in such speculation early in his ministry, as we can see from 1 and 2 Thessalonians (see especially 1 Thessalonians 4 and 2 Thessalonians 2), and the book of Revelation goes much further, using the language of Isaiah 65–66, beautifully portraying the divine deliverance of those marked for salvation but graphically depicting the fate of those doomed to destruction.

The New Testament also gives very great prominence to a biblical image that was becoming prominent in various Jewish communities, especially the community that produced the Dead Sea Scrolls. For Israel, God the Creator is One, and the creation is one creation. Powers that exist in the universe that are opposed to the will of God can only be accounted for as having their origin in the creative work of the One God. Late Jewish legend identifies Satan, therefore, as a fallen angel, the leader of an angelic rebellion in heaven, magnificently presented in John Milton's *Paradise Lost*. This Satan becomes very important for early Christianity, for he is able to help explain the presence of evil in the world, and especially to account for the refusal of Christians to accept the message of the Christ fully and to live by it. Satan also serves as the personification of all opposition to the will of God; as a spirit of dualism spread within the Christian movement, Satan can become the Lord of this present evil age, while Christ is the Lord of the age that is being born.

The Jewish community strongly resisted this leaning toward dualism. It spoke of an "impulse" (Hebrew, *yetser*) to evil and an "impulse" to good, present in every human heart. Evil arose, therefore, more within the human community than in the Godhead.

For both Judaism and Christianity, it is the prophetic visionary heritage that dominates. Jesus announces the coming rule of God, which he sees as breaking in upon the world even then and there. The people of Israel and the early Christians are all motivated to moral action on the basis of their affirmation of the rightness of the prophets' promises, and Christians insist that Jesus is both the bringer and the announcer of the fulfillment of these promises. Jesus dies on the cross, and Christians come to see in that death itself the truth of the prophets' promises. God's raising of Jesus from death is more clearly a sign of the consummation of God's work for Israel and for humankind; but for Christianity, the cross is the supreme indication of God's love for a good creation that has been bruised and damaged and corrupted by human faithlessness. God takes the side of the wounded and the struggling and the despairing and the lost, suffers with them, shares fully their lot. And God raises Jesus, God incarnate, signaling that triumph awaits all who share in this action of God.

THE IMPORT OF THESE PROMISES FOR ISRAEL AND THE CHURCH

Our task now is to suggest ways in which these visions of the Hebrew prophets and of Jesus and his apostles act to motivate and sustain our own moral commitments today. They do so, of course, as a part of our historical heritage. We are members of a community that believes these visions to be powerful depictions of what God wants from us. Since we want to please God and to avoid the divine displeasure, we will work to help realize these visions, to the extent possible to us as individuals and citizens and to the extent that our religious communities can do so. Indeed, we can understand these promises to be part of what God demands of us, so that they become part of Torah, the divine Law. Not to believe in and work for such a world would be disobedience. And as rational beings, we can see the desirability of a world marked by righteousness and peace, in which conflict among the various parts of the creation is reduced, and where the goods of earth are more equitably shared by all.

We have claimed, however, that there is some additional motivation lurking in these visions of God's purposes for the universe being brought to consummation. We see five features of this prophetic vision that summon us to moral action. The first is evident: It is a judgment not just upon us and our religious community but also upon our world. We feel the sting of divine judgment when we see our legal and social and economic institutions perverted for the gain of some. We know the sheer wrongness of a society in which the gap between rich and poor continues to widen. It is a crime against God's very ongoing purposes, against God's plans and dealings with the world, that the announced rule of God, which in faith we know is coming, is so long delayed.

These visions, in the second place, may give the community of faith enormous courage to hold on, to fail and try again, to keep confidence alive when the evidence is so strongly against the truth of these prophetic promises. Believing in God, we believe the truth of what the prophets and Jesus promised. God is at work in our world, we believe, to transform injustice into justice, to provide for the oppressed, the wounded, and the lonely. We should be working more diligently to do our part; but not all is failure and despair, for God does not fail.

A third feature of the moral import of these promises is how they impel us forward, lure us toward a more faithful life, toward greater acts of courage and helpfulness in bringing to realization the promises of the prophets and of Jesus. We live our lives out of the future, and the prophetic future beckons and draws us forward, sometimes even against our own personal inclinations. We are part of a movement, a cosmic movement, the end of which is blessing and peace with righteousness for all of the creation. This is why it is so important for the community of faith to teach this part of the heritage. Through our liturgies and sermons in temples and churches and through our study of this part of the heritage from earliest days through adult life, they become all the more a part of our envisaged future.

In the fourth place, these visions of the world made right and clean and pure are also visions of enormous aesthetic power. In every human being, it would seem, there is the drawing power of beauty, of fittingness, of aptness. Aesthetic truth informs moral truth. The purposed beauty of earth draws us forward to making the world, and our own moral existence, more pleasing, more fitting, more fair and beautiful. No doubt, the prophetic revelations are couched in unforgettable poetic speech and imagery for this very reason: to present to us not only a good world that God is bringing but also a beautiful world. Given the foulness and stench of much of contemporary life, given the appalling destruction of earth's beauty that humans perpetrate regularly, our hunger for a fair as well as a moral world is intensified, and to believe that God is bringing—with our help!—such a beautiful world is deep and sustaining motivation for the moral life.

Finally, we are moved to moral action by these visions because we, even now, share in their realization. While the new heaven and the new earth have not come, nor is Zion the highest of the mountains, nor is peace with righteousness a worldwide reality, even so, we partake of what the prophets and Jesus promised. We do so in worship regularly. We do so in the engagements for righteousness in which we participate, for there come those moments in which we know that what Jesus said is true: the rule of God is "at hand."

Indeed, the Jewish and Christian communities live now out of these promises, for they affect every feature of our moral life. This is not a merely spiritual affirmation; it is a description of what a life lived on the basis of the truth of the promises of the prophets and of Jesus actually means.

It would, however, be a base thing to be content to enjoy the communal blessings that the promises provide, turning our backs on the demand to continue to be in partnership with God, who is bringing these promises to fulfillment for the whole earth. Synagogue and church have certainly been tempted to do so throughout the centuries. The prophets and Jesus spoke of the public world, of the needs of human beings and animals and plants for life and care and nurture. The prophetic visions summon the communities of Jewry and of Christianity, therefore, to engage in the struggles for a better world. God will not fail. The One who called into being a universe so vast and complex and intricate does not abandon that universe.

Of course, it is no simple thing for individuals in our day to affirm the truth of these promises. We need the help of one another. We also need the visions of our own prophets and seers and saints. We share their faith and draw strength from their experiences. We seek to contribute our own faith and actions and insights for the good of the whole community.

As Martin Buber taught in *At the Turning*: "Creation is incomplete because discord still reigns within it, and peace can only emerge from the created. That is why . . . he who brings about peace is called the companion of God in the work of creation."[2]

SUGGESTED READING

Beker, J. Christiaan. *Paul's Apocalyptic Gospel: The Coming Triumph of God.* Philadelphia: Fortress Press, 1982.

Buber, Martin. *The Prophetic Faith.* New York: Harper Torchbooks, 1960.

Feld, Edward. *The Spirit of Renewal.* Woodstock, Vt.: Jewish Lights Publishing, 1991.

Gillman, Neil. *Sacred Fragments.* Philadelphia: The Jewish Publication Society, 1990.

Harrelson, Walter. "Prophetic Ethics" and "Ethics in the Wisdom Traditions," in *Westminster Dictionary of Christian Ethics.* Philadelphia: Westminster.

Heschel, A. J. *God in Search of Man.* Northvale, N.J.: Jason Aronson, Inc., 1987.

Kaylor, R. D. *Jesus the Prophet: His Vision of the Kingdom on Earth.* Louisville: Westminster Press, 1994.

Ogletree, Thomas W. *The Uses of the Bible in Christian Ethics.* Philadelphia: Fortress, 1983.

Tiede, David L. *Jesus and the Future.* New York and Cambridge: Cambridge University Press, 1990.

2. Martin Buber, *At the Turning* (New York: Farrar, Straus & Young, 1952).

GLOSSARY

Bet Din: a Jewish court that bases its decisions on Talmudic law.

CCAR: Central Conference of American Rabbis—the Reform rabbinical organization of North America.

Get: a Jewish ritual divorce.

Haggadah: the prayerbook used for the ritual at the Passover Seder (meal).

Halacha: the legal and regulatory portions of the Talmud, and of all Jewish lore.

Hebrew Scriptures: the 39 books in the Jewish Bible, sometimes referred to by Christians as the Old Testament.

HUC-JIR: Hebrew Union College-Jewish Institute of Religion—the Reform Jewish seminary that trains rabbis, cantors, Jewish educators, and social workers. The seminary has branches in Cincinnati, Los Angeles, New York, and Jerusalem.

Ketubah: a traditional Jewish marriage contract.

Leviticus Rabbah: a Midrashic commentary on the biblical book of Leviticus.

Midrash: Homiletic commentaries on every book in Hebrew Scriptures, divided into legal and ritual (*Halacha*) and floristic and anecdotal (*Haggadah*).

Mishnah: a compilation of legislation and interpretation of Torah principles edited by Rabbi Judah the Prince in about 210 C.E. The lengthier interpretations, expanding those found in the Mishnah, were compiled by the Jewish scholar ASHI in about the year 500 C.E. and are known as the Gemara.

Mishnah Torah: a commentary on the Torah written by Moses ben Maimon (Maimonides).

Pirke Avot: a section of the Mishnah that is a compilation of ethical and moral statements by many rabbis.

Talmud: contains both the Mishnah and the Gemara and often includes commentaries by later rabbis. The Talmud is considered to be the oral Law given by God, in contrast to the written Law, the Torah. The Talmud covers six basic areas of Law: Seeds (agricultural laws), Seasons (Sabbath and holidays), laws pertaining to the rights of women, Toets (civil law), Sanctities (laws pertaining to religious rituals), and Purities (laws regarding defilements).

Torah: the Pentateuch, or the Five Books of Moses.

UAHC: Union of American Hebrew Congregations—the North American organization of more than 800 congregations affiliated with the Reform Jewish movement.